God's Ex-Girlfriend

GLORIA BETH AMODEO

God's Ex-Girlfriend

A Memoir about Loving and Leaving the Evangelical Jesus

NEW YORK, NY

Printed in the United States of America
10 9 8 7 6 5 4 3 2 1

Ig Publishing
PO Box 2547
New York, NY 10163
www.igpub.com

ISBN: 978-1-63246-147-6

To O & S

If no one else ever reads this, I hope you do.

INTRODUCTION

"I think something was protecting me," my friend Josh said. He was telling me about the night he blacked out while driving and woke up in the pews of a church—a sudden break with reality at the wheel of a car, unprovoked by drug or drink.

I nodded gently, planning my response. I could capitalize on this. He was defenseless, the spiritual side of him splayed out, ripe, trusting and pliable. What better opportunity would I have to insert my worldview, to bury the seeds of fundamentalist dominion inside another person without them even knowing it? He was opening toward me like the mouth of a baby bird at mealtime. It was my mission as a conservative evangelical Christian to feed him the food of conversion.

"You were most certainly being protected," I said as I reached for my glass of white wine.

"You really think so?" Josh asked. "You really think something like God even cared?"

Exactly the kind of question I was hoping for. I had been taught how to control conversations like this, how to carefully drag vulnerability out of people and convert it into belief in Jesus Christ. I had been taught how to seem authentic about my life, authentic about my faith, generous in every aspect of my attention and time. People sought my friendship because they thought I was intriguing—a girl who believed in God but didn't judge their life decisions, who didn't chide them for being gay or getting drunk or having premarital sex.

I was not the type of fundamentalist Christian they were used to. I didn't picket soldiers' funerals or spout anti-abortion propaganda. They felt safe to share their spiritual ponderings with me, bouncing their unexplainable experiences off my open-minded perspective. I made them believe I was there to listen.

And I was, in a way. I was there to listen so that I could study them, learn my way into the broken parts of their hearts. The deeper I got, the more I knew my way around the caverns of their pain, the better I could tailor God's message to them. The easier Jesus could win their souls. Set up shop in a hellhole, my college ministry taught. New York City was my hellhole of choice.

"God cared more than you can imagine," I told Josh.

A month earlier, I had met with my pastor on the Upper West Side to discuss how I could subtly funnel all my friends into our church once Jesus was in possession of their souls. I had been a member of his small, forty-person congregation for a little over two years, active in all the ways I could be as a woman, which included singing worship, teaching children, and occasionally setting up snack tables.

"You have a heart for ministry," Pastor Luke had said at the meeting.

"Oh, yes," I replied.

I had at least a heart, maybe a few other organs as well. I'd converted to evangelical Christianity when I was nineteen, through the college ministry Campus Crusade for Christ—or "Cru," as they have since rebranded themselves. Cru taught me about the Great Commission, Jesus's commandment to make disciples of all the nations. Staff members trained me in evangelism tactics, in showing tract booklets to strangers on the street and befriending my peers over time, sharing the gospel slowly until it felt natural to them.

"How about starting a formal initiative?" Pastor Luke asked. "Like a Bible study for your grad school friends? A Bible study for skeptics."

It was a good idea. My friends in graduate school asked me about the Bible, and my faith in general, all the time—about how I thought it was the word of God, how I didn't date non-Christians, how I came to believe so radically in early adulthood, after growing up in a "cafeteria Catholic" family.

"Well, people might not show up at a Bible study right away," I answered, wanting to be realistic about our strategy in the battle for souls. "But we can start small, with intentionally spiritual conversations."

It was something I had been doing since my first day in grad school, since my first night in Manhattan, when my roommate Eleanor sat across from me and asked what I had done that summer. I seized the opportunity.

"I was on a mission trip," I said.

"Oh? What religion are you?"

"I'm a follower of Christ. But I'm more spiritual than religious."

I told her about my upbringing, how I was always longing for something, how I had been living with holes that could never seem to be filled by good grades or friends or boys. I told her about my old perspective on the Bible, how I used to think it was a load of crap, how I'd liked some of the teachings but considered it dated and a catalyst for violence, like what happened with the Spanish Inquisition. I told her about Jesus, about finding him in college, about reading the Bible with a different lens and learning that it was more relevant than I realized.

"I'm full now," I told her. "I have more than I could ever need."

"That's nice," she said, "but how are you full on something you can't see?"

The discussion continued, for many nights, many months. Exactly as I had planned, exactly as I had been taught.

So when Pastor Luke asked me to start a formal initiative, it felt like finally getting an official license for a business that I had been running out of my backyard. I was in New York to get a master's degree in creative writing, but Campus Crusade had taught me that my higher priority was spiritual. Everything I did was to be in service to Jesus, from the words I uttered in my classes to the parties I attended until four in the morning. I swore and smoked cigarettes outside of bars, developed an interest in craft beers to blend in with my peers. I drank alcohol to the glory of God, because, in the words of the apostle Paul, "I have become all things to all people, that by all means I might save some" (1 Corinthians 9:22). I was born for this mission, I had been told. I was a member of a holy priesthood, a family of warriors ordained by God to help him save souls.

On warm nights, I'd climb out the window onto the fire escape and pray, "Thank you for the fellow believers in my life. Thank you for making sure I'm never alone. Thank you for following in my footsteps, for going places before I do, for meeting me in my darkest moments." There I was, pursued by such incredible love. The love of God, the love of people. I'd be a masochist to give it up.

It took me seven years to realize that I had fallen into what was more or less a common American cult, and I spent four years running from it until I was able to start telling my story.

People often ask me how anyone in their right mind could convert to conservative evangelical Christianity. They don't phrase it that way, but that's how I hear it, because of my own guilt and regret about what happened during that period of my life. I often wonder how I could have been so stupid. I was nineteen years old, and I think I should have known better.

For a person who spends a lot of time explaining how many evangelical Christians I've known are intellectually brilliant, when it comes to evaluating myself, I still get caught up in the stereotype that all evangelical Christians are ignorant, brainwashed bumpkins.

That was not the evangelical Christianity I knew, nor is it a faith system I would have been attracted to. But it's a stereotype that I was well aware of before I converted, and it's perhaps a dangerous one, because I couldn't recognize the real thing when it came barreling my way. If I could be so sharply converted at the age of nineteen, what about others? Are people more vulnerable to this than we realize? If my story is any indication, the answer is yes.

I can't pretend it wasn't me who sat at a table with that pastor and plotted out a mode of evangelical control over the minds of New York City's young writers. I can't pretend it wasn't me who lied by omission to my friends when I told them I wanted to "catch up and grab coffee," failing to mention the fact that I was carrying tract booklets in case God emerged in our conversation. But I also can't pretend that I didn't turn away, that I didn't wake up from this strange dream. I can't pretend that I haven't been working to expose what I know about the heart of the evangelical movement, about the way it gains its converts, and, ultimately, its power.

1.

My first encounter with evangelical Christianity happened when I was six years old. I was in the basement of a church off a backroad in my hometown of Southbridge, Massachusetts, with a girl named Heather. She was growing up conservative Baptist, while I was growing up Catholic, with a priest who gave communion to gay people. I didn't know back then what words like *conservative* or *gay* meant, or why Heather's church might be different from mine. All I knew was that I liked Heather, even though she was a little odd and didn't let her hair grow long because she was constantly plucking it out from the back of her neck.

I had ended up in Heather's church basement after her mother invited me to attend a Christian children's function. My parents, thinking *Baptist, Catholic—same difference*—said yes, and so there I was, standing in a circle with a slew of other kids, dressed in mini wind suits and faded nineties' denim. The floor was tiled in big white squares that shrieked as our sneakers hit it, and the entire place smelled like a room where babies were kept, air fresheners in outlets to mask the smell of dirty diapers.

We passed a beach ball around, sharing one fact about God each time the ball landed in our hands. "His son died for us," one kid said, and the teacher nodded, following the ball around its loop. "He's a dad," another kid said. "He's God," said another.

When the ball finally got to me, I peered up and blushed. "He loves us," I declared, cheeks hot and itchy.

I gave the ball to the boy next to me, who took it from me quickly. "He thinks we deserve to die," he said, and passed the ball to his left.

I looked at the teacher, waiting for her to get angry. This jerk seemed like one of those kids who wasn't afraid of getting yelled at or punished. I had recently been introduced to this concept by a rambunctious second grader on my bus route, who drew boobs on one of the fogged windows and gave a cop the middle finger. But the teacher said nothing, as if the kid had stated a fact, no less true than the one I'd stated before him.

I was the type of child who scared easily. (Once, when a Halloween decoration on the outside of our house was stolen and my father remarked, "Ah, some clown took it," I became so afraid of clowns that I cried when one painted my face at a birthday party.) So when, in the basement of Heather's church, I watched an adult seemingly accept the sentiment that God thought we deserved to die, I was filled with a level of existential dread so great that I started openly weeping. I don't remember if anyone came to my emotional rescue, or if the adults attempted to explain this inflammatory statement to me, but I do remember asking Heather what she thought when we walked back to her mother's car that night.

"It's because we're sinners," she answered, small hands clasped below her jagged hairline. "We deserve to die, but he sent Jesus to save us." Thus was I introduced to the doctrine of salvation by a fundamentalist first grader, in the parking lot of her church.

When I got home, I sat on my parents' heavily pillowed bed, heaving tears as they tried to parse what was troubling me. I was in such a fluster that it took a while for them to understand, as I said things like, "He hates us!" and "I don't deserve to die!" When they finally realized what had happened, they were gentle but firm as they shared their perspective. "We don't believe that God wants us to die," they said, "and you don't have to believe it either."

There is something so warm about agreeing with your parents, like you've inherited something bigger than yourself. Being like-minded was all I could be without knowing anything else, and now, for the first time, I had to choose what to believe.

I decided that, as a family, we believed God thought we deserved to live. We believed in a God who would bring us all to heaven. Believing that God didn't want to kill me felt very, very good.

I used the light from my parent's television, beaming from their room under the crack of my door, to help me feel safe enough to sleep that night.

*

When I was young, I would tell my mother things like, "I remember heaven" as we watched my older brother learn to swim in the chlorinated YMCA pool.

"I know," she'd say. I'd told her the story before.

"I was an angel."

"Yes, you were," she'd agree.

My mother wasn't a stranger to supernatural claims. Her brother had died of non-Hodgkin's Lymphoma when he was eleven, and she said that he'd walked into her classroom as a ghost the day he passed. She could see through him as he sat on her teacher's desk, mouthing words she couldn't hear but which let her know he was okay. Her grandmother picked her up from school that afternoon, and her brother followed behind as they walked, tossing a football in the air.

"Were you scared?" I asked. I was sure that seeing a ghost would frighten me unconscious.

"No, no," she said. "It was peaceful."

I told my mother that I had seen God in heaven, and that he was bald and looked like a man and a woman.

"I'm sure," she said.

"He talks like a nice lady," I continued.

"That's good," my mother responded.

I imagined God this way, as the most comforting of creatures, a living hearth you could sit by forever. He was a father and a mother and he sometimes sent dead people back to their families to let them know they were okay. To believe he thought we deserved to die would have killed that God inside of me, a God created from my mother's stories and her own agile belief, a belief that said sure, I was a baby angel who remembered heaven if I said so.

But my mother's stories weren't always so comforting. I didn't know my father's side of the family because my mother claimed that they weren't good people. When my father wasn't home, my mother would feed my siblings and I chicken nuggets from the toaster oven and tell us that our paternal grandparents wanted to take us away from her.

"Why do Nonnie and Poppo want to kidnap us?" my brother Matt asked.

"Because they hate me," my mother said.

"Why do they hate you?" I asked.

"Because I don't want them to kidnap you," my mother answered. According to her, our grandparents were evil, and after they kidnapped us, they'd kill her. Our father would let it happen because he was scared of his parents and didn't want to get cut out of his inheritance. It was like a story from the soap operas my mother watched. We were too young to know that soap operas weren't real life, so my mother's explanations sounded plausible. My brother and I got to work on a secret plan of defense, watching *Home Alone* over and over and drawing blueprints for booby traps that only we could understand. We pretended to test them out by throwing bouncy balls down the stairs, and decided that if we got desperate, we'd launch rocks at our grandparents with slingshots.

Our father tried to tell us stories about his parents, too, about when he was a little boy and they'd go sailing on Lake Champlain, but we always interrupted and told him that we didn't want them to kidnap us. "They don't want to kidnap you," he tried to reassure us, but we didn't believe him. We thought he was in on the scheme. "We believe Mommy," we said, and watched him resign himself to a hopeless type of disappointment we couldn't heal.

He tried to give me birthday cards from my grandparents that were filled with money, in secret as we drove, just him and I. I'd tell my mother about it because I didn't know what else to do. "They're trying to buy your love," she warned. I gave the cards back to my father.

One time, my parents got in a fight while we were driving down a highway, a sunny day that made the car warm and my eyes squinty. It began abruptly, like all their fights, bursting out of what sounded like a calm conversation to me from the back seat. I didn't know what they had been talking about, or what they were suddenly shouting about, but the yelling got louder as the fight wore on—my father's voice shaking as my mother unbuckled her seatbelt and opened the passenger door.

"What the hell are you doing?" my father snapped as my brother and I started to cry. "Close the door, Mommy!" we shouted.

My mother leaned forward and adjusted her legs, one going toward the road.

"All right!" my father screamed. "Enough! I'll do it!"

And with that, my mother closed the door and fastened her seatbelt. As she turned on the radio, I wondered what my father had agreed to do. Whatever it was, I knew it had to do with our grandparents. And while neither of my parents ever spoke of the incident again, never sat us down to explain why she had opened that door or reassure us that she'd never do it again, I started to think about what preventing a recurrence would take—and if it had anything to do with me.

✷

My mother had forbidden us from knowing anyone beyond the borders of our immediate family—her, my father, my brother Matt, me, and my two little sisters, Emily and Gillian. But I was curious about the other people I was related to. I had a cousin named Jenny, who called me when I was six years old, the day before her wedding, to ask me to attend. "You better be there!" she said, her voice bright. "I have place cards made for both you and your dad!"

I knew I had met Jenny once when I was a baby, because there was a picture of her holding me that my dad kept in his dresser, her looking teenage-chic in a blue T-shirt and jeans, me a red-faced newborn. He had other pictures, too, that my uncles and grandparents had sent him—Jenny at her prom, Jenny graduating high school, Jenny and her fiancé in boats on a lake. She could be like an older sister, and there she was on the phone, wanting *me* at her wedding.

I told my mom I wanted to go.

"I'll still love you," she said. "But I will be very disappointed."

I remembered her trying to jump out of the car and I knew what disappointment looked like on my mother. I chose not to go to the wedding, like I chose not to take my grandparents' birthday cards, like I chose not to believe my father: for the sake of my mother's safety.

But the older I got, that more I questioned my mother and her reasons for isolating us. "Do you hate Dad's parents because yours are dead?" I asked her once.

"No," she said. "But I can tell you've been thinking a lot about this."

*

When I was eleven, my father told us that his brother would be visiting one day while my mom was at work. He said that he was tired of us not knowing our family and he hadn't told my mother but would deal with it if she happened to find out. We kept the secret because we wanted to know our uncle.

We went to a restaurant with a large taxidermy bear at the entrance, and I ate a hamburger as my uncle talked in a Donald Duck voice. My sisters were enamored because he was funny and playful, and they were little girls whose brains didn't yet work on as many tracks as mine. I was glad to be with him, but wary, and I wished we could stay at the restaurant. Instead, the plan was to go home and pick up scuba-diving gear. My mother was still at work, but I was afraid to risk it.

And indeed, when we parked in front of our house, there was my mother's car in the garage. As I'd feared, she was home, and had seen my uncle's car in the driveway.

She walked out the front door in her pajamas, no shoes. "Get out of the car," she demanded.

"No! my father responded.

"Get out of the car," she repeated. My father told her that we deserved to know our uncle, but my mother shook her head, repeating herself. "Get out of the car."

My father tried to drive away, but she grabbed the sill of his open window. He stopped the car, but it still dragged her, and the force of the brakes caused her to tumble down the road.

My sisters bawled and my brother's head was in his hands. I looked out the back window. My mother stood up, blood on her face, pajama shirt pulled up revealing bleeding breasts.

I dealt with the aftermath of my mother throwing herself at a moving car by going upstairs to study for a science test. I closed the door to the bedroom I shared with my little sisters, our beds stretched across three corners with mounds of dirty clothes between them, and read the necessary textbook chapters.

I didn't leave my bedroom until it was dark, at which point my mother had emerged from her room. She was still wearing her bloody pajamas, and the blood on her face had crusted around her swollen lips. Her left eye was swollen, too, bruised as big as a lime. She came up to me, gave me a hug, and kissed me on the cheek. "We're going to get through this," she said, and I wondered what that meant when she had done "this" to herself.

My uncle emailed a video the next day, which our father showed to us while our mother took a nap. "We're going to get your mother help," my uncle said on the screen of my father's computer, but we didn't. I knew we wouldn't—in fact, couldn't—because my mother didn't think she had done anything wrong.

✷

As I grew older, my imagination existed to help me cope with the fear that my mother would die. It also existed for my father, so I could be a part of the world with him, alive and okay, if only on the surface. It existed so I could build a world separate from my parents, one where I wouldn't have to be confused into anger by their actions. It existed so I didn't ask questions about things I couldn't change—my mother's sanity, her refusal to get help, my father's unwillingness to draw a line in the sand and do more to stop her from traumatizing us.

My imagination existed to protect me, but it grew threadbare with time, like an old sweater, and as the holes in the yarn grew wider, it needed a fix I couldn't get by believing in something on my own.

2.

My second encounter with evangelical Christianity occurred when I was fourteen, at a vending machine.

I was in show choir at school, and we were practicing a number in which our chorus teacher, Mrs. G, wanted us to take off white bathrobes to reveal sequined red dresses. The choreographer, her husband, planted large cardboard lollipops on the stage that we were supposed to pick up and hold with two hands in front of our chests. He asked us to sway until our mass of bodies formed a V-shape, and then bounce on our knees hard enough to make our ponytails twirl.

All this oddly seductive yet virginal configuring made me hungry, so I left the auditorium and went to get a Snickers bar from the vending machine in the teacher's lounge. I walked up to the machine with a dollar in my hand and saw my teenaged reflection in the glass—a face that had grown long with the onset of puberty, curly brown hair that was parted down the middle and tucked behind my ears.

Did I, in any way, look like Liv Tyler? Was I, potentially, the spitting image of an elven princess? I had recently seen *The Lord of the Rings: The Fellowship of the Ring* in theaters and felt like I had found my calling. Though I was now in high school, my fanciful inner world had not abated, and my imagination had met its match in a realm just as far-fetched, self-assured, and complex in its narrative makeup as the stories I had always created for myself. I went to work immediately on incorporating this world into my fantasies, mentally recasting the characters in my ongoing reincarnated-angel story, which by now involved the soul of the real-life Prince Harry as my angel lover.

In this fantasy (or very real and secret spiritual past, as I considered it), Harry and I were angel warriors who did battle against demons. We had been engaged to be married in the heavenly realms, but then we both died in separate battles and were sent to earth as humans who would one day find each other and save the world. Years later, I would come to understand that this was all, essentially, the plot of *Sailor Moon*. There was, of course, room for other characters in this story. I decided that seeing *The Lord of the Rings* made me remember other angels from my past. Liv Tyler, for example, resembled my big angel sister (hence the perhaps *striking* resemblance between us), and Elijah Wood looked like our father, who I decided was the archangel Gabriel. Viggo Mortensen *really* reminded me of Jesus.

While I was eating the candy bar, and, as I often did, hoping that Prince Harry had the faintest recollection of me from our time together in the heavenly realms, Simone Scott entered the room. Simone was one of the most arrestingly beautiful girls in our school—partially because she knew how to do her makeup and hair in ways I to this day don't understand. Once, on a chorus trip, she used a single elastic to give me a bun that made me look like I was going to the Grammys. She was a cool girl who didn't act like a cool girl, who spent time caring for the lowliest, most socially awkward cretins of our teenaged community like me, the type of young lady who thought that a visor with *Sea World* inscribed in rhinestones was the height of fashion. Simone was nice to people even I tried to ignore, like Lisa Carr, a small, shriek-pitched girl with a short haircut who always seemed to be screaming. I once saw Lisa fly through the air from the top of the chorus risers because some football players, Lisa claimed, had pushed her. Simone would calm Lisa, quieting her cries, soothing the demons that lived in her head as a result of her social abuses.

"How are you?" Simone asked me that day in the teacher's lounge. It was deeper than the typical *How are you*, because Simone always made it clear through her actions that she really wanted to know.

I made some fairly innocuous statement, and Simone related that statement to God and invited me to share my views on him. I hid my reincarnated-angel identity, because I didn't trust even someone as kind as Simone not to laugh at it, but I did acknowledge to her that reincarnation was definitely real. I also said people didn't go to hell; the whole idea was just a farce used by archaic religious oligarchies to make people do what they wanted.

"But people do go to hell," Simone said.

It was a surprising response. I had not experienced ideological pushback about my views on the afterlife in some time, at least not since my friend Heather and I were walking on the beach and she tried to convince me that I should read the *Left Behind* series of books to prepare myself for the Rapture.

"Okay, so people go to hell," I said. "Why?"

"Because they have to," she said.

"But why? Why do people need to go there?"

"Because God needs to send them there when they don't believe in him."

"That's not a good reason," I told her.

"Yes, it is," she told me.

It was then that Mrs. G walked into the teacher's lounge, probably to beckon us back to show choir practice, but upon hearing the word *hell*, she decided to voice her views.

"Oh, people go to hell," she said, taking a seat at the table with us.

I could not believe that Mrs. G was on Simone's side. Here was a woman making us dance around in bathrobes with towels on our heads, who openly said *fuck* and *shit* during chorus because she didn't know how to play the piano and always plucked out the wrong notes. And she was religious? I wouldn't have guessed.

"I get people going to heaven," I said. "I just don't get why God would send anyone to hell."

"Well, it's unbalanced if he doesn't," Mrs. G said. "You can't have a bunch of people in one and not the other. That doesn't make any sense!"

As we kept talking, a janitor entered the room, mopping the floor and attending to the garbage cans before piping up himself. "A lot of people are in hell," he said, resting his mop against the wall. The janitor explained how he told all the children about hell when he taught Sunday school on the weekends, and they intrinsically got it. After what had happened at Heather's church, this seemed strange to me. *I* certainly hadn't gotten it, intrinsically or otherwise.

So there I was at fourteen, defending my views of the afterlife against three people I hadn't even asked to have this conversation with. The discussion went on for a full twenty minutes before Mrs. G shut it down and said we needed to get back to choir practice. I felt like I had lost the argument, even though I was still the only one who made sense to me.

"You should come to church with me," Simone said as we left the room. My head still in a haze from twirling my own logic around itself, I considered it, if only to gain understanding on her perspective. I wanted to know how someone so kind could believe that God would send people to hell just because they didn't believe in him. What a petty God that would be. What a narcissist.

I went home that night and, once again, sat in bed with my parents, this time contemplative rather than in tears. I told them about the discussion, about the three against one, about how Simone had invited me to church and I was thinking of going.

"I don't think you should go," my mother said. "I mean, do you really need all that?"

What she probably meant was *Do you need to muddle up your mind with that garbage?* but what I heard deep inside was *You are already spiritually full.* I had a solid view of God that I had created myself, my own angels and archangels: my own religion, in a sense. Did I really need to know why Simone believed what she believed? I already knew it wasn't true, so how would it aid me?

Simone gave me her number, but I didn't call her, and she never asked why.

✷

Note to fundamentalist missionaries and evangelicals of all kinds: The above story is an example of a very ineffective way to convert a person. Below are the three major things that went completely wrong, and advice on how you can do better next time.

1. **Do not start with hell.** I repeat, *do not* start with hell. You are not members of the (deep groan) Westboro Baptist Church. You are cool-looking evangelical Christians, for heaven's sake! And cool Christians know how to talk nonchalantly about hell. They know how to cloak themselves in the nice stuff first, like love and forgiveness, and the purposefulness of a life in Christ. They get "John 3:16" tattooed in typewriter font on their arms so they can talk about how God so loved the world to strangers at coffee shops. It's called branding, people. Brand yourselves in love! Get people hooked on the good stuff first! Get them warm and comfortable in the idea that their lives have meaning, and then hell will be an easier trade-off in their minds.

2. **Don't gang up on anyone.** What are you, a bunch of bikers? Jesus sent missionaries out two by two, not three by three with a janitor and a foulmouthed choir teacher on board! I know it makes you feel all good and spiritual inside to be there together validating

each other's beliefs, like God orchestrated this moment by placing the three of you believers in this scenario together. But the person you're trying to convert doesn't see it that way. It is much easier for that person to believe that there are three brainwashed cult members in the room than that God is the mastermind behind the whole thing.

3. **Follow up about the church thing afterward.** After spiritual conversations, our data shows that only about 15 percent of convertees take the initiative to follow up about going to church. You may think you nourished a fig tree into bloom over the course of your thirty-to-ninety-minute talk, but you most likely did not. It's probably still a seed sitting in the ground, without the tending and encouragement it requires to grow. You. Need. To. Follow. Up.

I cannot tell you how disappointing it is for me to see you make these mistakes time and time again. You've got the spirit of God's only son living inside of you, but the world thinks you're crazy! Show them you're not. Show them what the love of Jesus can do!

Now, keep reading for an admirable example of a much more effective conversion.

✵

Cate became my friend during our freshman year at Fairleigh Dickinson University, a small private school in New Jersey I had chosen to attend because it offered me a scholarship *and* allowed me to dual major in Theater Arts and Creative Writing.

Cate and I took our first class together, a seminar about being freshmen. She walked into the classroom on the first day and sat behind me, casually cool in a Phillies shirt with three-quarters-length sleeves, hair so blond it was almost white. I thought, *Ugh. I don't get along with blondes.* I don't know where this judgment came from, as I hadn't had any particularly negative experiences with blondes. I think I just considered blonde to be the world's most coveted hair color, and because I was not one, blondes made me feel insecure.

In truth, I was insecure about every aspect of college. I was on a sprawling green campus in New Jersey, farther than I'd ever been from my family in Massachusetts. I was also a geek who wore a replica of Arwen's Evenstar necklace from the *Lord of the Rings* movies and still dreamed of becoming a famous actress, singer, and writer simultaneously. And after experiencing the ramifications of my mother's prescription pill addiction, I didn't want to do anything that would make me feel out of control—such as smoking, drinking, or having sex, all of which I assumed was expected behavior in college.

Even though I was eighteen, I felt like I was still thirteen, as I had grown up without having done what I had seen other people my age do—have a serious romantic relationship, experiment with alcohol, figure out who they were by trying to be someone completely different. I had given up Barbies, but I was still playing with dolls in my head through my fantasies. My worst fear was that someone would tell me it was time to stop.

And then, it happened.

During freshman orientation, a group of juniors made us play a game called "Never Have I Ever." When someone shouted, "Never have I ever had a threesome in a hot tub!" they all raised their hands to indicate they had. Feeling like this slew of sorority sisters had presented me a terrifying future on a platter, I headed over to the Office of Student Life after the game was over, and half in tears, desperately told the concerned adult administrator that I already hated college.

As I walked out of the office, another student followed me, introducing herself as Tara and ushering me into another room. She had been eavesdropping.

"You don't have to do any of those things in college," she said, and I felt the panic in my heart subside. "I'm the president of a Christian club on campus. We don't smoke, drink, or have sex. You should come to our welcome meeting!"

For many college freshmen, that description would have been the biggest turnoff in existence, but it was music to my ears. I put the meeting in my calendar.

✷

The club was called Campus Crusade for Christ. When I showed up, Cate was already there, her Bible open on the table.

I was surprised to see her at the meeting. As the blondest of all blondes, God's gift to the world of hair color, I thought she had a better shot at being accepted by society than I did with my high-waisted polka-dot capris and brown, over-moussed hair-mop. She could have been a normal college kid, who drank and did drugs, who was comfortable enough to hang out in frat houses without being afraid that the guys would call her ugly. Showing up at sexless Christian events was for people like me, who the outside world didn't want to touch with a ten-foot wizard's staff. Cate didn't need this, but here she was anyway, spending her time with a bunch of weirdos.

I looked around. There was Tara, who was also not bad looking, but had an air of disingenuousness about her; she'd told me that she loved me thirty minutes after we'd met. Next to her were three guys and a girl who I could tell were all very into anime. Across from me was a light-eyebrowed lad with a guitar singing the word "holy" over and over again in different keys with one eye on Tara, who was obviously the target of his crooning. Cate was the only person in the room who seemed regular.

I hadn't brought a Bible because I'd grown up in a Catholic world where Bibles were always provided, and besides, I didn't think we'd *actually* be reading the Bible. Instead, I had brought a comprehensive, 4,000-page list of drug-rehab centers around the country that I'd gotten from the library. I fancied myself a novelist and was inspired by James Frey's memoir *A Million Little Pieces* (though it had been exposed as a work of fiction). I wanted to write an edgy novel where the main character was a recovering drug addict, but since I didn't want to do drugs myself to find out what that experience was like, I had decided to do "research" instead by calling a bunch of centers in the book, which I had yet to do.

"What's that book?" Cate asked. Her first question to me.

"It's something I need to do research," I said, turning it around to show her the cover.

"Why are you researching rehabs?"

"I'm writing a book about a drug addict."

"Oh. What's it about?"

"A guy who used to do drugs."

She asked me what my favorite book was. I told her *A Million Little Pieces*, but also *The Lord of the Rings*. She told me that she loved *The Lord of the Rings*, too, and *Harry Potter*, and all of Dickens. She asked me if I wanted to see *The Chronicles of Narnia* with her, and I said yes.

✷

Cate and I became fast friends. She was like the blond-souled version of me. She liked all of the things I liked and introduced me to even more, like dipping fries in milkshakes and half-off appetizers at Applebee's. We binge-watched episodes of *Freaks and Geeks* on the weekends, eating cake and chicken fingers with tall glasses of grape juice. We ordered Domino's before Christmas break and played all three *LOTR* special extended editions in a row, laughing when Frodo put the ring on and closed his eyes because the DVD player made it sound like he was farting. We explored the campus when it snowed, our own little Narnia, taking pictures by lampposts and venturing out for gift-buying. We visited her parents on occasion, praying over dinner with her father, baking cakes with her mother. She became my cafeteria buddy, my sleepover companion. My home away from home.

I told her my secrets, the painful things that were hard to revisit. Cate learned all about my mother's anxiety, her paranoid fears, the migraine medication I discovered she'd been taking too much of, which caused her to stumble around the house and slur her words. She listened sympathetically, even though she couldn't fully understand. She seemed so cool compared to me, so much better adjusted, so much less emotional, with a pragmatism I envied. Cate was confident and stable and never seemed upset. I couldn't imagine her angry, or frightened, or sad enough to shed a tear.

One Sunday, I met her in the cafeteria after she got out of church. We sat with our chunky eggs and overcooked steaks, Cate dousing her plate with A1 sauce, which she taught me was the secret to making bad food edible. I asked her how church had been, and she said that it was hard, which was odd. Usually, Cate said church was "Awesome!" in a way that made me curious, if not a bit disconcerted. How could something as boring as church be *awesome*?

"Why was it hard?" I asked.

Cate took a breath. "Because the sermon was about death." She then told me about a friend of hers who had died in a car accident the year before. She wasn't sure if he was a Christian, which meant that he might not be in heaven. Most of her friends from high school weren't Christians, and she worried about their salvation. She moved the food around on her plate as she spoke, grabbing a napkin when she finished because she had begun crying.

Tears. Real tears. How could this be happening? Cate was logical, full of sense. She digested information like a recycling compactor and funneled it into different compartments, not stopping to take a look at how the bottles made her *feel*. I was the opposite. Every thought made me feel everything. I couldn't go to Bath and Body Works without getting emotional.

But here Cate was, crying. She really believed what she was saying.

"I'll spend the rest of my life trying to help them know Jesus," she said, stiffening back into her logical self.

I felt bad for her, but I also admired that she loved her friends enough to want to save them. However, I did not believe that Cate's dead friend was in hell, nor did I believe that her friends from high school would go there. Cate, on the other hand, grieved the possibility.

Poor, poor Cate, I thought. Crying over milk that wouldn't spill. If only I could reveal to her my secret angel mission to reunite with Prince Harry and bring peace to earth. If only I could let her know that hell was not a place people could go!

✵

While I felt immersed in Cate's world, at times, she could get distant —resentful, annoyed. When I didn't agree with or understand something about her worldview, she'd metaphorically lock me out and leave me banging on the door to get back in.

We sat on her bed one day and looked through a magazine. We flipped through underwear ads, and I pointed out one with a handsome man.

"That guy is hot," I said. "And probably gay."

"What?" she responded, eyebrows scrunched. "Why would you say that about someone?"

I was confused. She seemed to think I'd said something unkind. It was as if she knew the guy personally and I'd called him ugly or dumb.

"Well, he's a model," I said. "Isn't that . . . a thing?"

"No, it's not a thing. You should never think that about someone."

I wanted to question the legitimacy of her reaction. I wanted to tell her that being gay wasn't a bad thing. But Cate had an authority about her, an intimidating sense of judgement that she swung around when she was debating morality or anything that made her feel righteous. Something about it made my chest drop, my feelings about myself crumble. *She's more logical than I am*, I told myself. *What if I'm wrong?*

We'd fight about politics. She didn't think the current president, George W. Bush, was all that bad, but I had watched *Fahrenheit 9/11* and thought he was absurd.

"Why do you hate him so much?" she'd ask.

"Well, Iraq," I would say.

"It's complicated," she'd respond.

I stood by my dislike of him, but doubt lingered in my mind. Did Cate know more than I did? Did she understand something that I didn't?

I'd never had a boyfriend and had a general distrust of men, often saying things like, "All men are assholes!" and "The guys at this school suck!" But Cate had a sympathy for men, a soft spot of sorts, which she flashed like a badge whenever I'd get into one of what she called my "man-bashing moods." "You're so hard on them," she'd say. "How would you like it if people said those things about women?" She didn't sense something toxic in the world of masculinity like I did, didn't think anything needed to change. Was I making a big deal out of nothing, smelling something rotten in a clean refrigerator? Was *I* the thing that was rotten? Was I smelling myself?

Cate was able to take my views and place tiny bombs in them. They'd detonate when I was separate from her, making a mess of my mind. I'd argue her words in my head, but I always came back to the same feeling: that I needed Cate to approve of me.

Why did I need her to like me so much? Was it her confidence, her conviction, the way she spoke with an assurance that seared through our arguments? Was it the way she moved through the world, planting herself like a statue, unmoved by fears of the future or any force that could upend her life? Was it the way she seemed to care about everything lightly, touching forks and doorknobs and the shirts she pulled over her head with an understanding of their transience? Was it the focus I could sense she had on things beyond what mattered to me, the relief it afforded her to cast our world aside in favor of another? Did I want that world, too? Did I want to peer into it, just to see what she loved? Did I want to understand it, or perhaps love it too?

There was an attraction to other women that whipped through my mind, a bisexual identity I hadn't allowed myself to have. I was in love with her humor, her intelligence, the way she matched all the parts of me. She ignited something childlike in me, this need I felt to impress her, to make her proud. She had become a mother figure to me, one who—like my mother—lived in a different reality than the people around her.

When she wasn't patient, wasn't kind, questioned and vetted almost everything I said, I questioned myself too. During the summer between freshman and sophomore year, I didn't hear from her until the semester was about to begin, and I wondered if, for some reason, she needed a break from me. We had signed up to share a dorm room, and when she finally emailed me pointedly to discuss logistics (Who would bring the microwave? Did I have a mini fridge?), I decided to become her favorite roommate of all time.

✷

Two months into our sophomore year, I was still learning how to interact with Cate in a way that wouldn't lead to her questioning my perspectives or behaviors. As a result, I didn't say many of the things that came to my mind. When I did talk, I made my statements as inarguable as possible, such as "I like our couch" or "I'm going to buy groceries." One night, after we'd brushed our teeth and climbed into our respective beds, I thought of a different approach. What if, instead of stating an opinion, I asked questions and listened to her answers?

"Why do you think God sends people to hell?" I asked, and this time I welcomed her explanation.

It wasn't something Cate was expecting. Her voice cracked as she spoke, and she launched quickly into an explanation of the concept of sin. "When we sin, we're missing the mark," she said. "It's an archery term."

I wasn't understanding, so she pulled out a tract booklet.

"Can I share this with you?" she asked, the booklet shaking in her hand. I said yes, and she opened it to the very first page: a picture of a baby's hand wrapped around a large thumb. "God loves you and created you to know him personally," it said. "He has a wonderful plan for your life."

She went through the booklet with an attentiveness that made me attentive, a desire that made a dry sponge grow wet inside my head. She was doing this for *me*, she was talking to *me*. I was asking questions and she was answering them with patience. She told me things I wanted to hear and hadn't yet heard, a narrative both simple and complex, one that I could understand and wanted to understand, if it meant we would be better friends.

What I would later come to know as the Four Spiritual Laws were outlined in the booklet, one on each page. First, I learned, that God created me. He loved me and wanted a relationship with me. Second, there was one thing getting in God's way of achieving this goal: sin. He couldn't be near sin, and I, like all people on earth, was filled with it. Third, Jesus was the only way to bridge the gap between God and me. He died to spiritually cleanse me of my sin so that God could be near me again. And fourth, in order for Jesus to cleanse me, I had to believe in him. I had to give myself to him, and then he could fix me and make things right.

Did I feel broken? Yes, I did. Did I want to be fixed? More than anything, yes. I remembered my mother bleeding on the driveway, the cries coming from my sisters, my brother's head in his hands, how much I wanted to leave the car. I thought about the loneliness, the worlds I had to hide inside so I could try to make it better. "You grew up the way you did because your family didn't have Jesus," Cate said. "Your parents were so messed up because they didn't have God to guide them."

I considered all I had with Cate, a friendship in which I felt known, one that would get better and better if we shared the same views. I thought about how happy it would make her, how much more she would trust me, how I could alter my imaginary world to one that other people believed in too. I just wanted to be normal, like Cate. I just wanted her to love me like I loved her.

So I gave it a chance. I prayed a prayer with her about letting Jesus take control of my life and allowing him to make me into a new person.

If this is real, I told myself, *everything will change tomorrow. If it's not, nothing will happen. I'll wake up the same person.*

I woke up early the next morning and went to the cafeteria, where I put a heap of eggs on my plate and sat down to eat. I looked at the students shuffling around me in their sweatpants and thought, *All these people need to be saved.*

✸

My friends! My brothers and sisters in Christ! Behold the above story of a God-ordained conversion. Here are three things that were done absolutely right:

1. **Act normal!** If you are stepping into the spotlight of

ministry, it is important not to act like a brainwashed Christian mole person. As the great Pat Robertson of *The 700 Club* pointed out secretly to his television staff, nobody is going to want to become a Christian if all the Christians they see are the opposite of attractive! You have to draw people in, especially when it comes to a faith system that is stereotyped as antiquated and uneducated.

2. **Target people with the same interests as you.** We all know that geeks aren't going to connect with members of the lacrosse team, no matter how much they pretend to care about net sticks. Seeking out people who share your particular weirdness is the optimal way to find fertile ground in which to sow your Jesus seeds. Leave the jocks for the Christian Lacrosse Lovers Association. We have believers of all types ready to infiltrate any social setting; focus on the ones you can handle best.

3. **Leverage the traumatic pasts of your convertees.** This is the essential sweet spot of all evangelical ministry. It's a spot you'll have to work hard for, as most people bury their trauma, but that's why God created friendship—to give you emotional shovels! Get in there and start digging, past all the facades, past all the semblances of happiness they've created to cover their pain. Expose their inner illnesses and show them they need a doctor, as Jesus so wisely said in Mark 2:17, Luke 5:31, *and* Matthew 9:12: "Those who are well have no need of a physician, but those who are sick." Present Jesus as the best doctor for the depths of their agony, an antidote they can access through one simple payment, i.e., their soul.

And I have to say, brothers and sisters, the whole getting-distant thing was also a nice touch on Cate's part. Intentional or not, it really was effective. Once you've organically created a level of emotional reliance in a relationship, choking the roots a bit is an interesting method to find out if the plant will grow the way you want it to. It creates a question for the plant: What is most important to me? Continuing on my path of aimlessness toward ultimate death? Or figuring out what the Provider is telling me so

I can learn how to have life, truly and abundantly?

It is all in the name of Jesus, no matter how you get there. Remember always that God can use a crooked stick to draw a straight line. His aim is always to bring glory to himself, and his glory is our gain. When he's happy, he allows us to be happy.

3.

When I told my parents I had converted to a new belief system, we were all in a hot tub, bubbles popping up our backs and sides. We didn't have regular access to hot tubs; my parents had rented a room in a hotel by my college so that they could stay overnight and watch me perform in a production of Arthur Kopit's *Indians*. After my parents saw the play, I slept at their hotel so that I could eat the continental breakfast in the morning and swim in the pool.

I didn't know I'd be telling them about my conversion there in the hot tub, because I honestly didn't have a plan to do so. I was trying out a method I had just learned called "waiting on God." God would tell me when the time was right, when he had prepared my parent's hearts to hear a story I knew was going to upset them. Apparently, God told me to tell them in a hot tub.

"You accepted Jesus?" my father asked. "Well, I accept him, too."

"No, I accept him differently," I said, attempting to make a distinction between his Catholicism and my newfound radical Protestantism. "I believe now that he's the only way to heaven."

"No," my mother said. "No. Honey, that's not correct. That's not how God works. I *know* that's not how God works." She then told me a story I had heard a million times before, about her years as a nurse and all the people she'd watched die. Christians,

Muslims, Buddhists, they all died in the same way—many at peace in the same way, regardless of their beliefs.

I blockaded the alluring kindness, the sentimentality of her humanism. It was a trick of Satan, I had learned, to believe that all religions have the same end, to think that you can mash them up and form a holistic image of the real God. I didn't need to do that, because I now knew who the real God was. He was the God of the Bible, of the Old and New Testaments, who sent his son to Earth to be punished for the sin that was mine. My parents called themselves Christians, but they didn't believe the essential fact that the death of Jesus had atoned for our sins and therefore belief in him was the only way to heaven. If they were going to be real Christians, the kind that joined me in heaven, I had to tell them this and pray that God would convince them.

"I saw my brother," my mother added. "I know what the afterlife is. I know he's in heaven."

The eyes of my Jesus-born spirit rolled. Teaching them the truth was going to take a while.

✷

Part of becoming a newly minted evangelical Christian was having my conversion affirmed by other people, to make sure that my new belief was genuine, and the Holy Spirit had taken over my heart.

First Cate took me to a thirtysomething pastor with a bright, big smile like a Walmart sticker. He was part of a church near my college within the Christian and Missionary Alliance denomination Cate had grown up in. He asked me a few questions, the final one being, "Do you believe that Jesus Christ is Lord and Savior?" to which I answered, "Yes." It was that easy.

"Congratulations!" he told me, and welcomed me to the family, like I had just married someone—which, according to him, I had. I had married Jesus.

I was then passed off to a staff member from Campus Crusade. Her name was Michelle, and she would "disciple" me—teach me about the faith as Jesus taught his disciples.

Cate brought me to meet Michelle for coffee in the campus student center on campus, then walked out the door, leaving the two of us alone.

Did she bring me to make sure I showed up? I wondered.

I had previously met Michelle on a spring break trip to New Orleans for Hurricane Katrina relief work that Campus Crusade had organized—a trip that I took with Cate the semester before my conversion. Michelle was engaged to a man named Dave, which Cate told me in a tone that insinuated this was an accomplishment on Michelle's part. "He's godly," she told me. "That's really cool." While gutting houses, I had accidentally shoveled sand into a bin in such a way that it plumed up into Michelle's face. She coughed and sneezed while I apologized profusely and Dave wiped her eyes with a clean rag.

I sat across from her in the student center and remembered the moment from New Orleans, feeling like a fool for having done that to her. I wondered if she remembered, or if remembering would have mattered.

She wore chandelier earrings and sunglasses on top of her head, a purple pastel scarf wrapped around her neck. "Did you bring a Bible?" she asked me.

"Oh, no. I don't have one."

She pulled a Bible out of her bag, a paperback with a cross on the front, and asked me to open to a slew of verses. All were familiar from my Catholic upbringing. Romans 10:13: "Everyone who calls on the name of the Lord will be saved." Matthew 6:33: "But seek first the kingdom of God and his righteousness, and all these things will be added unto you." The verses sounded nice enough, vague enough, innocuous even. Words like *all* and *everyone* were so inclusive! This kingdom was for all people, not just some like I'd feared.

She had me open to John 14:6, and I read out loud. "Jesus said to him, 'I am the way, the truth, and the life. No one comes to the Father except through me.'"

"Do you believe this?" Michelle asked. "Do you believe that only Jesus can save us from death?"

"Well, yes, technically," I said. "But . . ." I told her my theory, inspired by my mother, about the philosophical meaning of believing in Jesus. People like my mother very much believed in Jesus, but didn't believe others would go to hell if they didn't. Could it be possible, I asked Michelle, for that type of belief to work, for eternal life to be less stringent than her all-or-nothing approach?

"No," Michelle said, like a stern slap. "Belief in Jesus as the *only* Lord and Savior is the *only* way to get to heaven."

She dragged my eyes to John 3:36: "Whoever believes in the Son has eternal life; whoever does not obey the Son shall not see life, but the wrath of God remains on him."

If I wanted this kind of community, this kind of protection, this kind of friendship with Cate, I wasn't allowed to believe anything else.

✷

The only option I had for my nonbelieving family and friends was to hold out hope, but hope, that tease of the mind, had long been the reason for my most devastating disappointments.

During my freshman year of high school, for example, I'd hoped I would get elected to the student council, even though I was unpopular and didn't know what type of promises to make in a speech. I went to the podium on election day and made a promise that mattered to me: I would rid the school of drug-based iniquity, starting by single-handedly flushing everyone's dirty cigarettes down the toilet. I didn't get elected, my hopes of making the school a no-smoking zone were dashed, and I cried for three days. Once the tears dried, I read the student council constitution and discovered a loophole that allowed me to join through a mere ten hours of community service. I did so, feeling slick. Popularity be damned!

I then set my sights on getting elected to a position on the executive board. I wanted to be the historian, because I knew how to work a camera, and I liked telling stories. I got my speech ready, one that didn't mention cigarettes or toilets, and went up against one of the most popular girls in the school, whose entire speech consisted of three words: "Vote for me." I lost, again, and decided that hope couldn't help me with anything.

Cate thought hope was worth having, though, and she had it in ways I wasn't sure I could. She had hope that her friend who had died without knowing Jesus might have still been in heaven, and that her friends who didn't know Jesus would come to know him before the end of their lives.

"How, though?" I asked her. "What does having hope for that even look like?"

"I imagine them as Christians," she answered. "I imagine what they'd be like as believers, and that helps me keep going."

The absence of hope, you might say, is anxiety. I say this from the part of my head that makes me late to work as I walk around the apartment and unplug everything from the outlets, check the bathroom faucets, make sure the stove isn't on. I lock the door, walk to the elevator, then walk back, unlock it, and lock it again. There is comfort in the repetition. I handled anxiety as a child by making bets with myself. *If I can make it around the roller rink five times before the clock says 1:26, I'll marry Prince Harry. If I can jump up to this tree branch in the next three jumps, I'll publish the book I'm writing about a kangaroo with magical powers.* If I could skate quick enough, jump high enough, I'd make a better life for myself. I'd have a stable family with a handsome celebrity prince. My mother wouldn't be lying in the road or taking sad naps in her bedroom—she'd be the mother-in-law of a royal, attending fancy luncheons in ornate hats.

This was how I pretended I could save my mother from herself, and save my family from her fears, from the rage she'd display if we fell out of her orbit. I could change the orbit, adjust the narrative, write a new story for our lives. If I imagined a different world with enough force, I could make it real, and we wouldn't have to remember who we were or where we came from. I realize now, much later, that I was always trying to save my family.

Jesus, Cate told me, was where my anxiety should go. I should cast my fears unto him, and he would take care of everything.

"But how?" I asked. I didn't know how to give a feeling to someone, as if my fears were a book or a sandwich that could physically be removed from my presence.

"You stop worrying." she told me. "You let him worry about it instead."

This felt close to impossible for me. I had spent my whole life using my worries as fuel to keep me moving toward a better future. My worries were essential to the survival of my dreams. To stop worrying would surely throw me into a morbid loop of stagnancy, and I would never get my mother—or myself—off the road.

"Trust him," Cate told me, over and over. "Trust him with the people you love."

So I prayed, an action that didn't make much sense to me either, and asked God to help me with my problems. I felt that, being omniscient, he should already know to help me with them even if I didn't ask, but Cate said prayer was my initiative. It was the way I showed up.

I asked God, "What would my family look like as believers?" I imagined, or he imagined, I wasn't sure which.

My father, a man whose loneliness felt palpable, cracking jokes at a Bible study with men his age.

My mother, no longer calling to make sure I wasn't dead,

raising her hands up at church to praise the God who saved her from herself.

My brother, filled with angst and depleted too early of innocence, gaining some of that innocence back for a future that would be so different from his past.

My sisters Emily and Gillian, too young, too little to understand, able to grow up in an environment filled with Jesus and people who loved him.

My family to the second power of themselves.

Hope was imagination.

✷

I went home for the winter break of my sophomore year a redeemed soul, a daughter of the King. I had confidence in my present and my future, because God loved me and was with me and wanted to use me to bring glory to his always-present holy self. I was a baby Christian, I had been told, still drinking metaphorical milk, not yet ready to eat the spiritual meat of the most difficult biblical teachings. Cate and my "discipler" Michelle were taking me through the Bible slowly, softly. I had a month off before the next semester, and I wasn't sure how I would grow in my faith without seeing them. Good thing Cate and I were spending the next semester in England together.

Back home, I went into the basement and walked in circles, praying for my family. My family came downstairs at different moments, disturbing my time with God, shattering my prayers for their souls.

One day, my sister Emily came down, coughing, sick with a cold that wouldn't go away. "What are you doing?" she asked.

"Nothing," I said.

"Are you talking to yourself?"

"Um, no. I'm talking to God."

"Oh. Okay, then."

She was fourteen, a high school freshman. She thought I was cool, a ruse I had managed to maintain since her birth. She listened to the most ridiculous things I told her and entertained them as real possibilities. When I sat her down years before and proclaimed that I was a reincarnated angel from heaven, she had a dream that a Jesus figure walked down a flight of stairs made of clouds and pointed to my sleeping body in bed, mouthing something she couldn't understand. She believed in me in my most unbelievable moments.

Her cold had started to sound like a bacterial infection, a crud that was trapped and committing acts of fission in her lungs. This wasn't something new; in family videos, she could be heard clearing her throat off camera, a sharp rumble, a constant state of pre-hack. When she was little, my parents were told it was allergies. When my mother brought her to the doctor this time, he thought it might be something else, something more serious. He repeated tests that had been administered when she was younger and sent them out to a large hospital. My sister, getting sicker, grew half circles under her eyes and started sleeping a lot.

One day, I heard the door open, footsteps plunking to the bottom of the basement stairs. It was my mother.

"Emily is sick," she said.

Well, yeah, of course. I already knew she had a cold.

"Come upstairs," she said.

✷

Cystic fibrosis is an overproduction of mucus, a disease of the stomach and lungs. It's genetic; when your father and mother both bring the gene for it to the table, you have a 25 percent chance of inheriting the disease. Most people with CF are diagnosed as babies, and they often don't live past the age of thirty.

Emily was fourteen when they told us she had it. Fourteen when we learned she had a terminal illness. I was angry. How could someone have a terminal illness for fourteen years and not know it? It didn't make sense to me that she could be so sick after being relatively healthy for all that time.

"She was sick when she was born," my mother told me.

I remembered being four and visiting Emily in the NICU. She held my finger, my whole hand stuck through the hole in the side of her incubator. The tubes attached to her face seemed to grow out of her like tentacles, like she was my new alien sister. I asked my father why she was in there, and he told me she would be all right—her lungs just needed some help.

Something had been lurking. I could admit that to myself. The cough that had been following her had finally caught up.

Before I left for England, I cried in my childhood bed. My sister was dying, and I was leaving the country for three and a half months. I wouldn't be able to stop thinking about her the whole time I was abroad. I would have questions that would only be answered through email, through phone calls on a pay phone in the basement of my English residence. How would I know if the medicines and chest-shaking contraptions worked, if the mucus in her lungs loosened, when I couldn't hear her coughs for myself?

"Should I still go to England?" I asked God. A serious question.

I heard nothing in the basement, felt nothing but the pang of a coin dropping inside of me. I'd already paid for my plane ticket. Of course I was going.

✷

I saw Cate in the airport rolling orange luggage, a pair of giant clementines filled with her belongings. *My sister in Christ*, I thought, rolling my green discount bags alongside her. I was proud to be seen with this person, this member of my new, problem-free family.

I wanted to forget about Emily's illness, even though I knew I wouldn't. I wanted to take the trip of my dreams and have Cate teach me how to put all my hope and sadness in God. I wanted the emotional escape that I thought my new faith promised me, a happy ending that the words "terminal illness" didn't offer. More than anything, I wanted to learn how to save my sister. I wanted to have some hope that if the worst happened, she would end up somewhere that I could go, too.

When we got to England and nestled ourselves in the masses of carefully trimmed shrubbery and little rivers that accompanied the roads, I told Cate about my sister. She approached the matter with logic.

"You know what the most important thing is," she said.

"I know," I responded.

"She needs to know Jesus, whether she lives until twenty or seventy. It would be better for her to die early knowing Jesus than to live to an old age never knowing him at all."

Cate told me that I needed to pray. Pray, pray, pray. She was obsessed with praying. "I think you'll feel some hope if you pray," she said.

We were living in a Jacobean mansion that our college owned, the face of their study-abroad program in England. It was in the parish of Wroxton, by the town of Banbury, and it was surrounded by thatched rooftop houses, fields, trails, and water. I went running one morning because it felt like something I should do amid so much beauty, not because I was the type of person who generally ran. I went down a path and looped around to a pond where swans floated, picking at their feathers, then continued on to a field of poppy-looking flowers that sat next to another body of water, this one with a waterfall.

A series of stones made a line across the pond. Stepping stones. Jumping stones. *God, do you want me to jump*? Someone said yes—was it me, or was it God?

I jumped, from one stone to another. They were wet, slippery, and I almost fell at the center. I stopped. I was standing in the middle of the pond. From a distance, it probably looked like I was standing on the water.

Show me that you love me, I said to God. *Show me that you're here. I need to know.*

I looked into the waterfall. There was an arch, I could see, buried inside. *A lover's arch*, I thought, my sight drawing above it. A rainbow grew from the water, from the top of the arch and beyond. That was my sign. He loved me.

✷

I went out and prayed in the morning fields. I cried in stone gardens that were covered in vines. My faith grew independent of Cate, tied to her conversational guidance but standing on its own now.

God spoke comfort to me through journals I'd take outside, scribbling my prayers in the pages and then letting him take over my mind, write through my hand—a form of prayer that felt so intimate I couldn't distinguish him from myself. I read his words alongside my own, awed at the love in his voice, at how he knew what I needed to hear. The Bible called him my Father, the ultimate lover of my soul, and he told me that he loved my sister, too, that he wanted to save her, that all would be revealed in time.

I told Cate what I was hearing from him, and she said the experiences were real, the words true. It lined up with his promises to his people in scripture.

✷

I expected hope to be anxiety's antidote, my ticket out of pain. I thought it was an emotional anesthetic, the means to carry me through change without having to feel anything. Hope would come and the anguish of my memories would flee, the sting of my sister's illness growing tolerable, like going to sleep hungry and dreaming about breakfast until it finally came. But hope is not Novocain. It's really nothing more than a wish. Hope is an inward image of things we want, things that will happen or won't. It may take the edge off the pain, like a couple of ibuprofens, but it's not a cure. It offers meaning, but not absolution.

I felt the evangelical God's hope come to me in a waterfall-drowned archway with a rainbow jutting out. I was looking for hope when I found it, needing promise, a sense of meaning, and there it was, tied to both life and death, God saying *I understand, I understand, I have experience with all of this*. I stopped wanting to know why my sister was sick, because I was given a mission: Tell her about Jesus, pray for his conviction, so she could know him and have eternal life. With me. In heaven.

4.

It took me a long time to form genuine friendships, the kind in which two people share an almost symbiotic understanding. From the ages of eleven to fourteen, I forced myself into the lunch table of the popular girls, because I couldn't imagine the possibility of a good future for myself if I didn't associate with the most admired people in my world, no matter how many times they told me, "Nobody wants you here!" By sophomore year of high school, they were so used to my presence that they didn't complain anymore. In fact, they were genuinely surprised, even a little hurt, when I decided to leave their lunch table in favor of another. One girl actually called me on the phone. "Why are things changing?" she said. "You're not sitting with us, we're in a new school. What's happening?"

"It'll be fine," I responded. "Change can be okay."

Ben, Morgan, and I became friends over a series of attempted interactions. Ben had sat next to me in sixth-grade health class, but when we started talking, a popular girl commenced the age-old chant about two people kissing in a tree. To avoid that ultimate humiliation, we didn't speak again for four years. Morgan and I were in chorus together, she an alto, I a soprano. In seventh grade, we took a school trip and traded songs we wrote on the bus ride over—hers a fast-beat, sassy tune about a guy who wronged her, mine a slow pop-princess ballad about Prince Harry being an angel. I thought her song was amazing and was so impressed she had written it. She, secretly, thought my song was terrible.

It wasn't until we were fifteen that we realized how similar the three of us were, that we were kindred in ways we needed. Ben and I recognized it in math class, switching textbooks so we could draw monsters with hidden penises on each other's paper-bag book covers. Morgan and I saw it at a writing conference, when the other students wrote dramatic poems about the disturbance of their souls and we couldn't stop laughing at their faux-profound art. The three of us spent the entire summer together—pool parties, movie nights, and cheap take-out dinners. We recognized the ridiculous in each other, the holes that needed to be poked until we learned how to fill them. We weren't afraid of tragedy, of each other's devastations. We were each other's advocates and confidants, the only ones who knew our whole stories. We were open, emotionally bare, in ways I didn't know how to be with anyone else.

✷

When Cate and I were in England, she introduced the concept of spiritual family to me, of our new genealogical connection through the Holy Spirit. She told me that when I accepted Jesus, something inside of me changed, and the family I had before took on a secondary role to the family I now had in Christ. Cate already felt like family to me, so I wasn't surprised about our connection. But I didn't like the idea of my earthly family needing to take a backseat to her. How would I get Jesus to save them if I didn't put them first?

I had been telling her about my mother's aversions to the teachings of our faith, about my father's dislike of the whole thing, though he was glad that I wasn't "on the back of some guy's motorcycle." Cate told me their reactions were normal, but I didn't need to keep adopting their opinions. Jesus had spiritually separated me from them. She pointed me to Matthew 10:35–36: "For I have come to set a man against his father, and a daughter against her mother, and a daughter-in-law against her mother-in-law. And a person's enemies will be the members of his own household."

"I think it's okay to stop talking to your mother for a bit," she said. "Take a little break. She's not healthy for you."

✷

That summer after England felt like an ocean. I floated between the days, attached to nothing but myself, grasping in prayer for some semblance of spiritual fulfillment. I called Cate to get encouragement, but she didn't call back. *She must be busy*, I thought. *I know she cares.* I didn't want to be clingy or burdensome. I was with my family, but I needed the type of family she was, the type that was connected to the depths I had discovered in myself. There were ancestral lines I hadn't identified, a faith-based family tree much greater than me, all its branches and leaves crying out that Jesus Christ was Lord.

I was never alone, Cate and Michelle taught me. God was with me in the darkest moments. This felt dark, this island of familiarity at home. I wasn't the same person—the person who was born into this family, who cultivated these relationships, who chose these friends. I was now to the second power of myself. I had evolved. I wanted them all to evolve, too.

✷

My sister Emily hadn't asked much about my conversion. I don't think she understood it beyond the idea that I was no longer going to a Catholic church. Our lives at home moved with added anxiety about her illness, her afternoons revolving around an electric vest that filled with air and shook her. She'd turn the television up loudly to watch *That's So Raven* or *Gilmore Girls*. One hand on a remote, the other on a nebulizer. Breathing in medicinal mist, adjusting the volume.

She entered the bedroom we shared one evening after dinner and found me writing in my journal, the scrawls of God coming out of my head, harried. *Trust me, trust me, all will be revealed in time*, I heard him communicating, and then, as Emily walked in, *Look out for fertile ground.*

She sat on her bed, like she had the night I revealed my angel family to her. "What are you doing?" Emily asked.

"Talking to God," I said.

"But you're not in the basement."

"He's talking into my journal."

"Oh. Wow. What's he saying?"

Sharing the gospel with Emily was easy, like feeding a hungry baby. It felt like food she was meant to have as I spooned it into her spirit. I told her that God had been writing to me about her, that he wanted me to tell her about how much he loved her, that he wanted her to hold on to him while she was sick, and the only way to do that would be to accept Jesus.

"But I already accept him," she said. "I think Jesus is real."

"No, you have to accept him in the way God wants you to accept him," I said. "You have to believe that accepting Jesus is the only way to get into heaven."

She paused, and a cramp of fear ran through me. A small voice in my head asked, *Am I telling my sister the truth?* The voice was like a staticky radio signal that extraterrestrials might pick up floating above our atmosphere, except I was floating above myself in the atmosphere of who I used to be, charting a course to who I was becoming. The signal came through in the background of my thoughts: fuzzy questions about what I was doing and if any of it was correct.

Later that night, I turned to the internet for direction, as I didn't have Cate to guide me on the presence of this voice. "What does it mean when I doubt evangelical Christianity?" I typed, and hit enter. Answers of all kinds came up, websites written by believers and atheists. Some said that doubt was the first step toward godlessness, others said that it would ultimately set me free from him. I was careful with what I clicked on. I didn't want to be led astray, nor did I want to get swept up in a soapbox preacher version of Christianity. I preferred the composed, fashionably clothed logic that Cate and Campus Crusade represented.

I kept scrolling until I found a more neutral position. *Doubt is normal*, one website said. *You have to let Jesus heal your doubt.*

I came to accept my doubt as something I inherited from my nonbelieving parents, just like Emily had inherited cystic fibrosis. It was sewn into my blood and I could see it in theirs when I shared the gospel and they rejected what I said. "You can't tell me that a good person who happens to be Muslim is going to hell," my father said while I held the tract booklet with which Cate had converted me. "I saw my brother," my mother repeated as I sat at the foot of her bed, trying to explain that ghosts are just demons who are trying to confuse us away from God. I'd come by my doubt naturally, but I knew better than my parents, with their blatant, painful rejection of God's truth. I saw that inborn doubt in myself, but I would rise above it. I would defeat this mental disease I had inherited, because if I did, then I could help them defeat it, too.

✷

Emily agreed to come to church with me. In a sensible move for a fourteen-year-old, she wanted to explore the faith more before handing her soul over to Jesus.

This meant that I had to find a church near our hometown. Since becoming a believer, I had only been to churches with Cate in New Jersey, and I didn't know what the spiritual landscape was like in Massachusetts. Southbridge boasted six different Catholic churches, one for each different European immigrant population that settled there in the 1900s, and a seventh for the growing Puerto Rican population. Anything that wasn't Catholic, even inching near evangelical, was a little weird—like Heather's church, or the one that Simone had made a weak attempt to bring me to in high school. Weren't there any cool churches with handsome guitarists covered in purple stage lights? Pastors who wore ripped jeans, muscle shirts, and Converse sneakers? Those were the kinds of churches I liked and wanted to be at.

Coincidentally (or God-plannedly, as I told myself), I reconnected with an old friend from high school on Facebook named Lauren. We met for ice cream and she told me about her boyfriend, whom she had met in high school and was still dating two years later. I saw a chance to plant God-seeds and told her that I didn't have a boyfriend because I was waiting for God's best.

"That's great!" she said. "You know, I'm saved now, too!"

We nearly screamed with the ice cream cones in our hands. Sisters in Christ! After all these years apart, we had come back together with the greatest thing in common! I asked her where she went to church, and she told me she was a member of a Baptist congregation two towns over—a thirty-minute drive to a little white chapel. Her boyfriend's family attended, along with about twenty other families—a modest size. Perfect for Emily's introduction to Jesus.

The next Sunday, Emily and I stopped by Dunkin' Donuts for iced coffees on our way. I wanted her attention propped up by caffeine at her first *real* church service. We arrived at the chapel and sat in the wooden pews, similar to but smaller than the ones in our Catholic church. It felt comfortably familiar as the congregants waded in, carrying babies and expressing excitement to see each other and Jesus.

Lauren sat with Emily and me. "I'm so glad you're here!" she said. I was glad we were, too.

The service began with a good-looking, olive-skinned man in a gray suit playing a guitar and belting, "In Christ alone my hope is found" with what sounded like the voice of Christ himself. People stood and sang with their hands in the air. When my own right hand floated toward the ceiling, Emily glanced over, peripherally, curious. The pastor came out in a tweed sports jacket and delivered a message about the importance of putting God first, how he wouldn't let his sons play football games on Sunday because "Sunday is the day for the Lord, and my family will be devoted to him on this day." I liked the stringency of the message. Cate would approve, I thought. I had found a place she would have taken me herself.

For the rest of the summer, Emily and I would grab coffee and drive the thirty minutes to Lauren's church every Sunday, blasting the Rocket Summer until we pulled into the silver-graveled parking lot. Parents would play with their children on a swing set next to the chapel, building castles in a sandbox, chasing them barefoot on the grass.

"I wish we grew up like this," Emily said one day. "Wouldn't it have been nice to have all these people around?"

She was getting it! I just needed to show her that it wasn't too late—this could still be our family.

I wanted to connect with people at the church, find the kindred spirits that Cate told me about when we were in England. One day, I brought Emily to a pre-service Bible study where we met demure women and men with grass-stained jeans, all their faces deep in their Bibles. They greeted us, but didn't seem interested in getting to know us. I wondered if they questioned who we were—two strange girls showing up to their church without parents.

Lauren attempted to introduce me around, but her boyfriend's mother was the only person to take an interest in me beyond my first name. She invited Lauren and me to meet her at her office one evening, after work hours, where she served us Girl Scout cookies and Styrofoam cups filled with hot water. We dunked bags of Earl Grey in our cups and I asked about her work.

"We talk to women who are pregnant and want to abort their babies," she said. "We tell them what their other options are."

Oh, I thought. I hadn't encountered an organization that did this before.

She went on about the evils of abortion, how she could show me videos to prove it was murder. "They go in with a suction tube and suck the baby out," she said. "And you can see it in these videos—the baby is swimming away!" She also told us about how her oldest daughter, as a child, was possessed by a demon and started scaling the walls of her bedroom. "I can say this for sure: the devil is real."

From abortion to demon-possession, she moved on the doctrines of salvation. "You know why you're saved?" she asked me point-blank.

"Because I prayed to Jesus to save me?"

"No!" she said. "It was nothing *you* did. God chose you before time. You are one of his elect."

I disagreed with her. It didn't make any sense that God would choose some people to be saved and not others. How could he deem anyone deserving of hell if he himself had forced them away from believing in him?

"You believe that God is in control, right?" she asked.

"Of course."

"Then that means he's in control of our choices and our salvation."

This, I realized, is what my new family believed—a theological system I would later come to know as Calvinism.

✷

Emily and I kept going to the white chapel. We kept trying to connect with the congregants, but found ourselves mostly ignored. The pastor kept up with his heavy-handed sermons, speaking loudly about his desire for the community to evangelize more. "What about the people you work with? Your neighbors? Are you telling them about Jesus? Are you bringing them here?"

The people in the pews bowed their heads, nodded.

What about us? I thought. *Do they know my sister is sick? Do they know how much she needs to know Jesus?*

I encouraged her to make friends on her own. Maybe I was the one holding her back, maybe she could do better without me. After the service one day, I nudged her in the direction of a group of girls her age, all awkward-looking in brown dress-overalls and Crocs. I stood off to the side, pretending to look for someone.

She came back to me a few minutes later. "I'm done," she said.

It felt like junior high again, trying to wedge myself into the lunch table with the popular girls. Despite our efforts, we couldn't enter this family.

"This isn't God," I told Emily as we drove home. "This isn't how God's people usually act."

"I just don't feel comfortable there," she said.

"Let's try one more time. And if something doesn't change, then we won't go anymore."

The last time we went, the pastor went all hellfire and brimstone. "If you're not saved, that means separation from God!" he said. "And God hates sin. So you know what that means."

When I went back to school, I told Cate about the whole saga.

"I wish I knew how bad it was," she said. "I would have called."

She told me that God's people aren't perfect, that they're sinful like anyone, and they fail sometimes, too. She told me that the people at the white chapel had treated us wrong. I felt validated—a sense of healing, like a wound was being sutured.

Why couldn't my sister have a Cate, too? Why couldn't she have been introduced to the gospel in an environment like Campus Crusade? Why did her first experience have to be so negative, such an antithesis of what had drawn me into the faith? I was angry. That church could have helped save her. They could have been her family when I wasn't there. But they weren't.

"Your first experiences weren't the best, either," Cate reminded me, referring to the stories I had told her about Heather and Simone. "And God still brought you back around to himself."

I learned later that the evangelical church sees itself as a human body—not one building, but an entire mass of organs, as the apostle Paul wrote in 1 Corinthians 12. Christ is the head, and all the churches fall beneath it, some making up arms and legs, others forming skin or lungs or veins. They work together for the glory of God, doing what the head tells them: walking, running, painting pictures, building houses. They admit that they malfunction, like body parts sometimes do. They get diseases and infections, and they sometimes need the antibiotics of prayer.

I thought that Lauren's church had failed my sister because they were sick. They had contracted some kind of isolation virus, one that made them play with only themselves. But I realized that it was no different from the way my mother treated our own extended family or the way the popular girls had treated me when I tried to sit at their lunch table. It was a human virus, one that evangelical Christianity had the potential to wipe out of our systems. If we did what Jesus told us, we wouldn't act like that anymore, which was perhaps the most mesmerizing promise of all.

5.

After the summer at the white chapel, I went back to college hungry for more Christian training. "I want to learn how to evangelize," I told Cate. "I need something better than just sharing the gospel through a tract."

The gospel was the gospel, Cate told me. It was meant to bump against people's sin, which made it, in some ways, dangerous and offensive. But still, she said, there were ways to make it more palatable.

Tara had graduated, so Cate was now president of our campus Cru. The group was registered as a club with the Student Government Association, meaning it could receive financing and organize school events, just as legitimately as the French club or the chess club. Our branch also had an "executive board" that took care of the money and led the members in its mission—which was, ultimately, to convert all students on campus.

Cate asked our friend Hannah to be vice president. Our friend Leigh didn't exhibit any particular talent with money, but was nevertheless made treasurer. I, a new believer but already strong in God's word, was given the role of secretary. How emotionally redeeming to be *handed* a position in a club after all those years of struggling to get one on the student council. Maybe was God whispering, *This is where you will be able to effect change.*

Cate held a board meeting to plan out events for the semester. We met in a room little bigger than a closet on the bottom floor of the freshman dorm building, on couches that Cate and Hannah heaved in while I was auditioning for a production of *The Heidi Chronicles*. Hannah, Leigh, and I sat there and listened as Cate told us what she thought we should do.

Movie night was first on her list. I was familiar with Cru's version of this event. Tara had organized one during my sophomore year, screening *Seven* in the freshman lounge, where the youngest, most vulnerable students meandered and played cards. We'd arranged the chairs into a makeshift movie theater to create a comfortable environment for passersby to stop and watch. After the movie was over, with everybody's brains still shivering from watching Brad Pitt and Morgan Freeman discover rotting corpses, Tara stood up and asked questions about God on a microphone. "Why do you think gluttony is a sin?" Not a great question to ask a crowd of students you've been feeding free snacks and soda all night.

Cate felt that Tara's approach was too harsh for the sensitivities that nonbelievers at our school—and nonbelievers in general—had concerning Bible-believing Christians. She didn't want to scare people away. She wanted to attract them, show them how wondrous and beautiful our faith was. She wanted to help people see God the way she saw him.

"Let's watch *The Chronicles of Narnia* this year," she said. "And then I'll give a talk about the similarities between Aslan and Jesus."

Perfect, we all agreed.

Next up was an event known as Pizza and God, which was popular among many Cru chapters, Cate said. It involved buying a bunch of pies, putting them in a room, and inviting non-believing students in to eat for free. As Cru members, we'd be present to support Cate as she asked the group spiritual questions. Did they believe in God? If not, why not? If so, who did they think he was?

And what did they think about things like heaven? This would give us a chance to understand the spiritual climate, to get to know who might be receptive to the gospel, whose heart was ripe for seed-planting. It could also inspire people to ask *us* questions for a change, which would, in turn, give us a chance to talk about the real, living God.

"Only one change," Cate said. "Let's not call it Pizza and God."

"Why not?" Leigh asked. "I mean, that's what it is."

"Because God is a *term* to people. It scares them away."

Cate was correct, which I affirmed as a new believer: "I mean, if this was a year ago and I didn't know you guys, and you came after me with pizza? Talking about God? I would've thought you were weird."

"Then let's call it Chill and Chat," Cate concluded.

She was, in so many ways, brilliant.

✷

I started going to monthly regional meetings, labeled "Jersey Cru" by the staff members, because they were attended by Cru movements from campuses all across the state. It was hosted at larger universities, like Rutgers or Montclair, in auditoriums big enough for two hundred people, bands leading us in worship onstage. It felt like a special kind of church that met once a month on Thursdays, with cool hymns and cool clothes and only people my age. Even the Cru staff members, many of whom were married with children, looked like college students. Big backpacks, torn jeans and sweatshirts, Converse or flip-flops.

One Thursday, the lead staff member preached about "blending in" like the apostle Paul says he did in 1 Corinthians 9: "To those under the law I became as one under the law . . . that I might win those under the law. To those outside the law I became as one outside the law . . . that I might win those outside the law . . .

I have become all things to all people, that by all means I might save some."

"Paul tells us in this scripture," the staff member said, a distressed military-style cap atop his head, "that we must become like those we're ministering to. We have to look the part in their environment."

I looked at the staff and students around me, all attractive, all blending in perfectly to our environment. No disheveled soapbox preachers here, only the good-looking cream of the crop. We were being taught how to convert a whole college, an entire nation.

"Everything you're doing is for the glory of God, as long as you're doing it with the goal of leading people to him," the leader said.

It was about target audiences, I've come to realize through my current career in advertising. How do you sell something to a person, to anyone, to a world? Segmentation, the advertising world says. Break them up into pieces. The young. The elderly. Ages thirty-five to sixty-seven. People who wear chain bracelets. Millennials with hair loss. If our target audience was bohemian, we'd have pulled out the peasant blouses. If our target audience was burners, we'd all have gotten dreads.

But our target audience was college students, and college students tended to be liberal. So we ended up looking and sounding as liberal as they did. I don't think it was our intent to *pretend* to be liberal, but it was something that happened as a result of our blending in. We didn't want to associate with anything our target audience would reject, like legalistic dogma, or even the word "religion." Religion was rules and regulations. Religion was meaningless ceremony. Religion was hollow chanting and knee-shattering genuflection. We called ourselves "spiritual" to align ourselves with inclusivity, to make people feel like their ideas and beliefs were welcome in our world. Every event we put on, every activity we partook in—from class to chorus to student government to athletics—involved attempts at spiritual conversations. If I wanted to be act in school plays, sharing the gospel with fellow theater students had to be at the forefront of my mind. We were not living for ourselves. We were living for Jesus. Our lives weren't our own—we belonged to him.

✷

Cate, Hannah, Leigh, and I attempted to start a buzz on our small campus about an upcoming Christian magic show at Montclair State University. We posted flyers and talked about it with everyone, slipping the show into conversations as naturally as possible.

"What are you doing this weekend?"

"Seeing a movie. How about you?"

"Nothing really—but next weekend, I'm going to a magic show."

"Wow. A magic show."

"Yeah. You should come!"

This is how we hoped to entice people to witness the Christian magic of Brock Gill.

Christian magic may sound like an oxymoron, and in many ways, it is. In church, in Cru, and in every other evangelical circle I joined, I was warned away from Ouija boards and believing in ghosts, from summoning spirits and accepting Wicca. Even keeping a Buddha statue in my dorm room was outlawed. "People go straight to heaven or hell, period," Cate said. "Any spirit you see is a demon, no matter who it pretends to be." I was therefore surprised to hear that a Christian *could* be a magician, but I was learning that Christianity made itself into a sticker that you could slap on secular things as a holy qualifier. Rock music could be evil, but not *Christian* rock. Get me some Relient K, or Newsboys in concert. Yoga was derived from Hindu practices and rooted in the worship of false idols, but not *Christian* yoga, which put the *real*

God at the center. Let's all *shavasana* in the name of the Father, do our downward dogs with the Son lifting our hips.

Brock Gill's magic shows were designed to lead people to Jesus. I didn't know how he was going to do it. I imagined him casting a Holy Spirit spell, the audience transfixed by the sight of a wooden cross as he threw lights and colors around it. Somehow this Christian magic would change the hearts and minds of non-believers. Cru staff considered it the best shot we'd have at leading people to Jesus all year.

On the night of the show, we drove to Montclair with no non-believers in tow. No matter. The Cru students at Montclair had sold hundreds of tickets, enough to pack the entire auditorium with non-Jesus-knowing ears. Our presence was still needed, of course, to pray with people when they accepted Him.

Brock Gill had an upturned nose and thin, serious lips, a face so long that the tip of his head almost seemed pointed, eyebrows covered by shaggy blond bangs. This eyebrow coverage obscured his facial expressions onstage as he made cards appear out of nowhere and sent doves flying out of hats. He was funny, putting the audience in stitches as he shoved ping-pong balls in his mouth. "They've disappeared! It's magic!" he said, his voice muffled. He let us know throughout that what we were seeing was an illusion, until the end, when he told the audience about the greatest truth of his life: Jesus.

Upon hearing the name of Jesus, people began walking out. Brock continued his monologue, rattling off the spiritual laws, as people exited the theater.

Eventually, the only people left in the auditorium were Cru members, staff, and Brock.

Tricks are only necessary when you have something to hide. It's a magic *trick* because the magician conceals the true mechanism of action. In a way, tricks tell a bit of truth, if you look them in the eye and stare them into submission. There is an unwanted fact behind every misdirection, a reason that the trick is being used in the first place. With gimmicks like the magic show, Cru tricked people into hearing the gospel because we needed a soft landing, both for them and ourselves. We needed their eyes to say, *I'm not frightened*, so we could believe it too. The trick was the actual truth. We were afraid of what we were saying. We were afraid of the implications. We were afraid of our own God.

God makes us fail sometimes is what I came to believe, a knowledge that sat so deep it became an instinct. I learned that faith-sharing attempts could frequently go against the best laid plans, because it wasn't about our will, or my will. It was about God's.

✷

I went to Panama City Beach, Florida, for spring break of my junior year, where I learned about the differences between initiative evangelism and relational evangelism.

Initiative evangelism, Cru taught, was walking up to strangers with tract booklets, getting them to hear the gospel of Jesus and asking them to say the prayer at the end in hopes they'd convert. Relational evangelism was much more time-consuming, as it involved befriending someone and sharing the gospel gradually, through actions and words.

I realized that relational evangelism had been practiced on me. Cate had planned to convert me, and I didn't even know it. I had been converted under the guise of friendship, had fallen victim to ulterior motives. But was I really a victim, if the motive had been to save my soul? To introduce me to a God who could alter the state of my family if he wanted, heal my sister if he wanted, give us eternal life if he wanted?

If he wanted, if he wanted. It would all happen if he wanted. We could lead the horses to water, but only God could make them drink. God had made me drink. Had I been used? Had my friendship with Cate been a giant ploy to gain another follower, one who would multiply herself by using the same tactics on others? Had I been manipulated? Was I a big win?

No, I told myself, even though a part of me felt it was true. I swallowed the questions like old gum when there's no trash can around. I buried them where they couldn't be felt or seen, because I loved Cate, and I didn't want to argue with her. I had already been down that road.

✷

We went out two by two onto the beach of drunk partygoers, MTV cameras fixed on boobs and bikinis while we dressed in khaki shorts and two crew-cut tees each, to avoid any sign of cleavage.

I listened as Cate asked people survey questions. "On a scale of 1 to 10, how interested are you in knowing God?" If people answered 7 or above, we were supposed to walk through the "Knowing God Personally" booklet with them.

When it was my turn, I felt people's doubt inside myself as I approached them, Cate praying silently beside me that all hearts would turn fertile.

I walked up to a girl in a stringy, black-and-white-striped bathing suit. She was holding a green drink in her hands. She hugged me when I said hello.

"What's your name?" I asked.

"Tina!" she responded.

"Okay, Tina. Want to do a survey with me?"

She agreed and I went through the questions with her.

"Do you believe in heaven?"

"Oh yes," Tina said.

"What do you think it's like?"

"It's here!" Tina laughed, arms flailing in the air. "We're in paradise!"

I asked her how much she wanted to know God, and she responded with a resounding 10. I shared the tract booklet with her, and she nodded.

"I accept! I accept Jesus!" she yelled by the end. I settled her into a prayer, and she burst upon the word, "Amen!"

"Jonathan!" she screamed, running to the water. She jumped into a tan man's arms, her legs suctioning around his body. "I met Jesus!"

God works in mysterious ways.

✷

My brother Matt didn't seem to believe much in God, but he did believe that Kurt Cobain had been murdered by an electrician. He explained it to me one weekend when we were in high school, home alone with our sisters while our mother ran errands. We had busted through her parental control code (0000) and were watching Korn and System of a Down music videos over bowls of boxed mac and cheese. He'd read a book that said Cobain must have been attacked by the electrician because the angle from which he was shot would be impossible to achieve with a suicide. A botched police investigation was to blame for his death not being ruled a murder; it was "obvious" that someone had covered their tracks.

"But why would anyone want to kill him?" I asked, only a peripheral Cobain fan.

"Jealousy," Matt postulated. "Maybe money, too."

My brother was different from me, no matter how much I wanted to be like him. I had that familial desire to share his opinions, share his views on the world, but I couldn't bring myself to act like him—to see the world from his perspective. We shared the same childhood, were partners in both joy and trauma, but we internalized it all in opposite ways. I looked at our family, at the mistakes of our parents, at the isolation and anxiety, and said, *It's broken. I will fix it.* Matt looked at it and said, *It's broken. I will see it as it is.* He was the realist I wasn't, that maybe I couldn't be as I built my elaborate fantasy worlds.

He didn't care about school and didn't like most of the teachers, skipping math to hang out in the band room because he found more of himself in music. He grew his hair long and parted it down the middle. He taught himself bass guitar, wore Zildjian shirts and baggy jeans. He made friends with other guys who liked Slipknot and Deftones, smoking pot and occasionally drinking—nothing too dangerous, but enough to make our mother suspicious.

She became convinced that he was a heroin addict. She even planted a syringe filled with saline solution on the living room floor to prove to my father that Matt needed to take a drug test. My father, finding the syringe and completely buying the idea that a junkie would leave heroin on the ground instead of actually using it, stood over my brother's shoulder as he urinated into a cup.

Matt was always angry. For having a mother who wanted to send him to rehab when he didn't need it, for having a father who could potentially let her. For feeling, at the age of sixteen, unprotected. He thus decided to do whatever he wanted, because our mother would think the worst of him regardless. He bought a cell phone, which he kept hidden because my mother forbade them after watching an episode of *Dateline*. He spent the night with girlfriends against my mother's wishes. He stayed out as late as he wanted, got as drunk as he wanted, lived with an amount of furtive abandon that I couldn't muster as I sat through my all-honors classes, in my imagination-buffered life of reincarnated angels.

By the time I gave my life to Jesus in college, my brother was twenty-five and still living under our parents' roof. They were asking him to pay rent or move out. I felt bad for him, as God would never ask his children to leave, but I also knew that God had commanded children to honor their parents. What would my brother look like as a Christian? Knowing Jesus was the ultimate answer, the solution to the conundrum of his existence, but how would I get someone so angry, so cynical, to believe in something so mystical?

It's not my job, I reminded myself. *God is the one who changes hearts.*

I decided to do what Cru taught me: start evangelizing without letting people know that you're evangelizing. Relational evangelism. At the last Jersey Cru meeting before winter break, the staff members played a video in which celebrities talked about loving Jesus, to remind us that even the most famous of hearts could be turned to God's son. One of the people in the video was Brian "Head" Welch, an ex-member of Korn. My brother loved Korn! I went back to my dorm and scoured the internet. Yes, it was true—Welch was a Christian. Better yet, he'd written a memoir, titled *Save Me from Myself: How I Found God, Quit Korn, Kicked Drugs, and Lived to Tell My Story*. My brother needed to read this book. Korn would undoubtedly lead him to the Lord!

I got back to Massachusetts and drove up to Barnes and Noble two days before Christmas, praying the whole way: *Please God, please let them have this book.* I went inside and zipped right to the nonfiction section, searching all the way to the W's for God's best chance at saving my brother. They had one copy! Clearly, this was a sign that God wanted to save my brother. If there had been five copies, it wouldn't have been as big a deal—five copies would have meant God's saving grace was as cheap and easy to find as a Pizza Hut coupon. It wasn't. Jesus said that getting into the Kingdom of God was like a camel passing through the eye of a needle. Finding one copy meant that a camel would be threaded through a mother-fricking needle that Christmas.

I gave the book to my brother as we opened gifts on Christmas morning, saying casually, "I saw it and thought you would like it."

"Brian Welch!" he said, turning it over to read the back. "Cool!"

I saw the tricks succeed about as often as they failed, but I was taught not to view any result as final. "Sometimes we're just planting seeds," Cate the great gardener said, metaphorically tending potential pumpkins in all of her classes, at Cru events, and in every friendship she made. *Are we lying?* I occasionally asked myself. *Are we lying when we act like we don't have an agenda?* I learned that the Old Testament character Rahab lied to hide Israelite spies, telling the king of Jericho, according to Joshua 2:1–6, that the men had already passed through her father's property. A lie could be righteous, all the commentaries said, if it was in service to God.

My brother read Welch's book within five days of receiving it. He texted me his thoughts on New Year's Day: "It's the best book I've ever read."

There was hope for my family yet.

6.

When I told Cate that I had dabbled in Wicca the summer before college, she was shaken and more disturbed than I expected. "Have you prayed about it?" she asked. "Satan gets a foothold through that stuff."

I hadn't yet discovered past actions that needed to be prayed away. I'd entered evangelical Christianity, in my eyes, pretty clean. I was the most virginal of virgins, a professional volunteer who had once gone to New York City for a ONE rally, and not because it was founded by a famous person like Bono. I genuinely cared about humanitarian causes!

"How would he get a foothold?" I asked, frightened.

"It's witchcraft. Things like that are in his realm."

"What else does he have in his realm?"

"Pretty much any type of worship that isn't centered on God."

Cate told me that Buddhism and Hinduism were evil, that most Eastern religions and spiritualist parlor games were purposely alluring because Satan was trying to seduce people away from God with things that sounded nice to believe in but weren't really true. Reincarnation? Female gods? A deck of cards that spelled out my future in symbols? It was all a way for Satan to leech himself into my mind and make me doubt that God was the only one who had the answers I sought.

"But I became Christian *after* Wicca," I told Cate. "Doesn't that mean I'm cleansed of it?"

"Not necessarily," she answered. "There may be aftereffects."

Darn it, I was poisoned! Why had I walked around that stupid circle counterclockwise with my friend, chanting, "Earth, air, fire, water"? Now I had invisible thorns to dig out of my invisible soul.

The more I learned about Satan, the more I hated him. He was an angel who had caused a rebellion in heaven and taken, according to Hebrews 12:22, a third of the other angels with him—a story that struck a familiar, almost innate tone to me after years of fantasizing that I was a reincarnated angel who had battled demons created out of this event.

But evangelical belief introduced a twist: the battle continued on earth! Satan's main goal now was to destroy the souls of humanity, as God loved humans and Satan was jealous of them. He would try all types of tricks to lead me away from believing in God's truths—truths like "I am fearfully and wonderfully made" and "God has a great plan for my life." I was afraid that I was ugly. I heard the words in my head all the time. *Your thighs are too big. You're not pretty enough for a lead role. Your hair looks like a Chewbacca wig.* If that was the voice of Satan; he had always been with me—in the corners of my thoughts, sitting on the self-esteem he had stolen.

When I told Cate about this, she said, "God's plan for your life must be too big. The enemy wants to stop you before you begin."

That was what she taught me to call Satan. The enemy.

I was no stranger to enemies. As a child, I had an imaginary enemy instead of an imaginary friend. I remember daydreaming her up. With a small piece of chalk, I drew a strange-looking continent shaped like a foot on a blackboard. That was where she lived. I decided that she was the most terrible person in the world, and if she was going to have a name, it needed to be the most terrible name in the world, a name that I hated more than my own, a name that encapsulated her evilness.

Bis, I thought to myself. Gross. Her first name would be Bis. But what about a last name? Like a fart on the wind, it came to me. *Tone.* She was Bis Tone.

Bis Tone followed me around, frowning, dressed in black pants and a red turtleneck. She had black hair that was cut into an ugly, perfectly symmetrical bowl cut, and skin so white it was almost translucent. She was the cause of most of my problems. Stepped on a toy? Bis put it there. Got pudding on my shirt? Bis made it fall out of my mouth.

My brother Matt loved a good Bis Tone confrontation. When things around the house were too quiet, or if I was just irritated, I would yell, "Bis is doing it again!" and he would come running.

"Where?" he would ask, searching around the room. "Where is she?"

"There!"

I would point, and he would start attacking. He'd throw Bis in the air, body slam her to the ground, grab her by the ankles, swing her in circles and let her fly into the fireplace. Then he'd wipe the sweat from his little brow and say, "She's gone."

As I got older, I acquired many more enemies—classmates, roommates, people playing loud music in apartments below me. They have been both real and imaginary, recognizable and faceless, and they have all held my anger in the ways I needed when they arrived. They became outlets for the things I could not express as a child for fear of upsetting the delicate balance of my mother's world. I could not make my mother bear my anger, so my enemies bore it instead. These enemies became fallen angels, Lucifers who wanted to destroy me.

When evangelical Christianity gave me Satan, I no longer needed or wanted human enemies. Humans were broken, and it was my duty as God's child to see them that way. No matter how annoying or rude they were, no matter how poorly they treated me, no matter how many people they hurt or crimes they committed, my duty was to show Jesus to them, because humans were not the enemy—Satan was.

"Don't celebrate anyone's death," a Christian friend on my Facebook feed wrote when Osama Bin Laden was killed and people poured into the streets of New York City and cheered that the world was rid of him. It was the evangelical Christians I knew who were calling for an end to the applause. They believed that Bin Laden needed Jesus, and that Jesus wanted him. How could I not believe this faith was the truth, when it created a level of compassion that seemed like it could save anyone?

✷

After I became a Christian, I learned that bad things happened in one of three ways.

First, they could be my own doing. I was a sinful being, which meant that I couldn't help but screw up and bring spiritual trouble upon myself sometimes. For example, I liked to vent about people I didn't like (which Cate referred to, pointedly, as "gossip"). My freshman roommate, a non-Christian who liked to watch *Roseanne* on her tiny box set until four in the morning, once said to me, "Everyone thinks you're so innocent, but I always say you can talk shit with the best of them." That was not a flattering depiction of a young Christian woman, but it was how my roommate saw me, which was my own fault. I had fallen prey to the sin of gossip and slander; I had created that perception of myself, *by myself*. It would be that much harder to lead people to Christ if they saw my sin instead of Jesus.

Second, bad things could be Satan's doing through me—but this was sort of complicated. Satan was a wily monster, but he only had so much power over me now that I'd asked Jesus into my heart. If I fell victim to Satan's temptations, which always involved steering my mind away from God, I wasn't *really* a victim—just a weak-minded, sinful creature. Example: My Italian teacher was gorgeous, with sandy blond hair, muscled arms, and the face of Hugh Jackman as interpreted by a classical Greek sculptor. He travelled to campus from New York City, a motorcycle helmet attached to his leather satchel. I imagined him handing me a test back with a note on it reading: *100%. All correct. Meet me by the closet outside after class.* There, no words would pass between us, just sounds, quiet and hushed, as we made love. And then I would wake up from my fantasy, still a virgin, but now full of sinful lust. Satan had done it again! He had whispered the sexual thoughts into my mind and led me down a treacherous road of fantasy!

Third, bad things could be God's doing through Satan. There was no knowing why God allowed unfortunate events to happen, but all we had to do was look at the book of Job to know that God had a hand to play in some seriously nasty stuff. In fact, the whole ordeal with Job seemed to be God's idea, as evidenced by the business meeting between God and the evil one, when Satan asked God to let him mess with Job's life:

> And the Lord said to Satan, "Have you considered my servant Job, that there is none like him on the earth, a blameless and upright man, who fears God and turns away from evil?" Then Satan answered the Lord and said, "Does Job fear God for no reason? Have you not put a hedge around him and his house and all that he has, on every side? You have blessed the work of his hands, and his possessions have increased in the land. But stretch out your hand and touch all that he has, and he will curse you to your face." And the Lord said to Satan, "Behold, all that he has is in your hand. Only against him do not stretch out your hand" (Job 1:8–12).

Job went on to receive boils and plagues, to watch nearly his whole family die, to lose everything he loved, but he continued to praise God, to find his hope in him, no matter how many of his terrible friends stopped by and told him that this was all his fault. He knew that it wasn't. He knew it was God's doing through Satan, and that gave him some peace.

God wrote the final narrative, even if my body grew boils, even if my whole life burned down and my family perished. It was mysterious and more than a little disheartening to know that the lover of my soul would allow this type of pain, but I was assured by Cru, by pastors, by Cate, that I would understand it all in heaven. I would be able to ask my questions someday, and my eternal soul would be satisfied with the answers.

In one part of my mind, God did not receive the reputation that a literalist reading of the Book of Job made him deserve—a God in cahoots with the murderer of souls, a God who gave the green light to Satan before he tore a nice man's life apart, all so he could say, "I told you so, Satan." But in the predominant part of my mind, that was not a criticism I allowed myself to entertain. I needed God to be good, all the time, because how else would my family get saved? Nothing good came from me—all good was because of God. "And final thanks to God," I wrote in my bio for every play I performed, for *Pride and Prejudice* and *The Seagull* and *The Rocky Horror Picture Show*. "Without you, I would be nothing."

If I didn't praise God for the good things, I was afraid I would lose him. And losing him, naturally, meant losing good things. I was bound to give him credit, and each time I gave him credit, a piece of me washed away. Autonomy, identity, the actions that made me *me*. I was not my actions, Cate and Cru said. Jesus found me dead in my transgressions. He wanted to make me more like him, and that meant giving up my pride. That meant thinking *I can't do anything well on my own. These are the talents of Jesus. I am living on borrowed talent.*

Borrowed talent. Borrowed energy. Borrowed days. Borrowed life. If I left him, I'd lose everything, because he owned everything I was.

✷

Cate and I encountered Satan on a cool spring night at a church near campus, where we attended a Christian college group called The Loft. I curled the ends of my hair before going because I saw Cate do it and realized that maybe we would meet our husbands there. A group of good-looking, godly guys always showed up in leather sandals, saying "Dude! Grace, man! God is good," and hugging each other.

That night, when the Bible study portion ended and we were all eating snacks off small paper plates, Cate asked if she could speak to me in the hallway. I followed in the hush of her footsteps, which tried to communicate a normalcy her voice didn't. Once we were out of the room, she turned to me, and I saw the worry, the fear, the sorrow—but also a sense of adventure, of being caught up in something much larger than herself.

"There's something wrong with Brianna," Cate said. "And I think it's demonic."

Brianna was a freshman who had recently joined our Cru chapter. We weren't sure if she really knew Jesus or was just needed some friends. She seemed to agree with all the right teachings. When Cate handed a blank check across a table at Bible study, one that was made out to "Death" in order to illustrate how Jesus paid our penalty by dying on the cross for our sins, Brianna nodded her head in apparent agreement. On our spring break trip, she seemed excited about sharing tract booklets but didn't know who C. S. Lewis was or how to flip to Romans 6:11 in a Bible. Still, we accepted her as one of our own.

That night at The Loft, she started talking to herself, then ran downstairs and began walking wide circles in the parking lot.

I headed outside with Cate to evaluate the situation. Was Brianna having some sort of a psychotic break?

"No," said Cate. "It seems like Satan."

"Why?"

"Because it happened here. It happened at a church."

We went out into the parking lot and saw a pastor at the entrance, his white-gray hair short in the back and spiked at the tip of his forehead. He stood cross-armed, legs wide, Converse-clad feet planted, watching Brianna.

"What's she saying?" I asked the pastor.

"It's mostly incomprehensible," he said, "but I keep hearing 'no.'" Luckily, he added, a prophet was on his way. He was conducting a service at the moment, but would deal with the demon when he arrived in an hour.

"Let's pray," Cate said, heading over to Brianna. I walked behind her, lightly. We prayed that God would protect Brianna as she fought to prevent the demon from taking over, which we assumed she was doing every time she said, "No."

She then pulled a cell phone out of her pocket, and we watched her dial. Who was the demon calling? Brianna held it to her ear and didn't say anything, then put it on the ground. We promptly picked it up.

The screen said *Mom*. A woman's voice cried from the speaker.

Cate told Brianna's mother what was happening. Brianna's mother said that she needed her medication and asked if it was in her bag. Cate, rolling her eyes, instructed me to go upstairs and see if there were any prescriptions in Brianna's purse. I did as instructed, but found only a wallet, a planner, and some gum.

Brianna's mother wanted to drive to the church, but Cate told her it wasn't necessary—we would take care of Brianna and bring her back to the dorm.

We continued to walk in circles with Brianna, to sit when she sat. We followed her into the rooms she wandered into, onto the altar of the church. Before the prophet arrived, we were sitting with her in a pew. "I'm tired," she finally said, and we knew she'd found her way back.

We called Brianna's mom and let her know that some of her friends were bringing her back to her dorm and would make sure she took her medication. Cate and I stayed to give the prophet a report, to process our first demonic experience with someone who was more in tune with that side of spirituality than we were. We were told to wait for him in the nursery and we did, sitting on the ground like little saplings who needed water, waiting for a caretaker to come and nourish us in ways we couldn't do for ourselves.

The time that passed before he entered the room was a blur of thoughts, of questions, of my own internal fight with a more metaphorical demon.

She had a mental break, the demonic version of me said.

Sure, godly me said. *A Satanic mental break.*

Come on, demonic me snorted. *She has diagnosed schizophrenia.*

Well, maybe schizophrenia is from Satan, godly me retorted. *You ever consider that?*

Before I could answer, the prophet was already sitting in front of me, his belly rolled over his belt. "You're like Ruth!" he said, referring to the Old Testament character who followed her mother-in-law Naomi into another land after their husbands died. "You used to follow Naomi, but now you follow God!"

I didn't know how that was relevant to anything. If I was Ruth, maybe Cate was Naomi. Maybe I had followed her first. Maybe this prophet knew that, and then saw my independence from her. Maybe he saw my relationship with God and thought, *She's solid in her faith now, like a sapling grown into a tree.*

But I was not independent from Cate. I was tied to her just as tightly I was to God. They were one and the same to me. She felt like a parent and a partner, and who is God if not that?

Maybe prophets see what they want to see. Maybe we all do in any given moment. Maybe we want to see demons when we see schizophrenia. Maybe we have imaginary enemies because we can't recognize our real ones, because it's too painful to be failed by the people who are supposed to protect us. Sometimes enemies are about anger, about manifesting pain, but they can also be about self-criticism—they give wrongdoing a face other than our own. They take what we cannot bear and turn it into something separate from ourselves, something we can walk away from. Maybe in this way enemies can be our friends, when they pay for something that is ours by being cast into the fire. Or maybe we are just holding them hostage.

7.

Emily told me that our other sister, Gillian, cried herself to sleep at night. Happy little Gillian, twelve years old, was weeping into her pillow until she was unconscious. Emily said it was because of our mother, because Gillian couldn't make her stop taking the pills. I learned that both Emily and Gillian had had separate conversations with our mother, about when she began taking the pills (for painful migraines, when she was in her mid-twenties) and why she took so many (she was a nurse, she said, and knew how many she should take). I learned that while I was at college, my mother had begun losing her footing. Alert at work but high at home, she'd stay in bed most of the day, tripping down the stairs to pour herself a glass of Diet Coke.

"Gillian's afraid Mom's going to die," Emily told me.

"I am too," I said.

"Yeah, but imagine being around it all the time. You're at college. We actually have to see this."

It was true, and I knew it. I was absent, living a different life at school. I was entrenched in my classes, my plays, my mission to help Jesus save the whole world from itself. I could be selective when it came to hearing and thinking about my mother, calling my family or not, controlling my visits so that I could mentally survive. My sisters didn't have that luxury, and I felt guilty about that. I felt guilty that they were facing something alone when I, even with all my prayers, couldn't help but look away.

*

Cru is, in many ways, an organization of strategic empathy. Conversion starts with being able to empathize with someone's lived experience, with sitting beside them in their pain, staring at it together until it recedes. Trust is born that way, and Jesus seeds will only thrive in trusting soil.

But when it came to empathetic evangelism, our majority white staff team had their limits. It was because of this that we were asked to raise support for our brother in Christ, Trevor, at one of our monthly Jersey Cru meetings. "We want to bring Trevor on staff, and we need your help," Stuart, the lead staff member, said. "Trevor can reach people who I simply can't."

Stuart was white, and Trevor was black. Stuart was looking for a way to convert more people in the black community. His whiteness, he explained, naturally hindered his ability to evangelize to black people. He didn't know what it was like to be black, to live in the body of a black person, to live in a society in which inherited, systemic oppression influenced people's interactions, mobility, and life trajectory. It was strangely progressive for 2008, before words like "intersectionality" reached the mainstream, back when white America thought it had healed itself from racism by electing a black president. Here was Stuart, acknowledging the fog of privilege that rolled in and obscured his understanding as a result of his whiteness. He was an equal opportunity evangelist, and he needed another way into the hearts—the trust—of black people. Trevor was it.

By "raise support," Stuart meant for us to give money. It was something the staff members from Cru did—they fundraised their entire salaries. I learned that it was typical for a ministry organization to abstain from offering staff members salaries, that "depending on God" for income was a blessing in itself. The staff claimed to grow in their relationship with God by asking people to pay them in the form of monthly recurring donations. Not everyone was equipped for direct ministry, the logic held, but everyone was called to ministry, and that meant sacrificing time or resources or both.

I took a look at my bank account, which was funded by my work-study job at the college library: $200. I wrote out a check for $100.

I understood Stuart's call for diversity, and I wanted to support it. I wanted to see all people saved from hell and in a relationship with their creator. We were the most diverse region of Cru that existed—with the majority of our student body being black, Hispanic, or Asian—and the white staff members reminded us of this all the time. We represented the world with all the cultures we brought into that room. A lily-white church, they told us, was not what God had intended. He called for every tribe, tongue, and nation. We needed to help him deliver on that.

But I realize now that it wasn't about inclusivity, or intersectionality, or spiritually rescuing people of different cultures. It was about obliterating those cultures and turning them all into one: evangelicalism, with the evangelical version of God reigning supreme. It was a colonizing theology, focused on saving souls from damnation by conforming those souls to its thinking, its politics, its lifestyle. It was about homogenizing, popularizing an inherently white way of thinking. There is power for white people in that.

So the white staff members worked to indoctrinate people of every background, using people of color as conduits to correct their failures of relatability. And I, a white person, gave $100 to help it happen.

*

I made an attempt at helping Gillian through her emotional turmoil over my mother by offering up some Jesus while driving her home from dance class. It was January, and I was on holiday break, which gave me a mere month to plant Jesus seeds in the minds of my family members.

"Are you worried about Mom?" I asked.

"Yes," she said.

"Me too."

Silence followed. She clearly didn't want to talk about this.

This was not unusual for Gillian, the youngest member of our family, a whole seven years younger than I was—an eternal baby in the eyes of us older kids. Before she turned one, Matt, Emily, and I babysat her on summer breaks while our parents worked, putting her in a red walker and flinging her down the kitchen hallway as she giggled. When she got older and gained proper control of her appendages, she tried to keep up with us. We'd run to the slides at water parks, Gillian trailing behind, yelling "Wait! Wait!" as her little legs flew.

She didn't want to be left behind, and we didn't want to leave her behind. But as one of us, she was expected to fend for herself, to make sure she ate her fill of pasta before the rest of us got to it. There was much to keep up with—snacks, couch territory, possession of the remote control—in a home of four children who spanned ten years in age. Somewhere along the way, Gillian learned that it was easier to be quiet than to scream like the rest of us.

"What do you think the solution is?" I asked, trying to open her up.

"I don't know."

"I think it's Jesus."

Silence again. She was giving me zero leverage to make my case.

I thought I might get her interested by talking about how fun evangelical church was, like going to a concert every Sunday and hanging out with all your cool friends.

"What do you think about church?" I asked.

"It's church."

"But do you have fun there?"

"No."

"Do you want to?"

A shrug.

I was failing, and I knew why: she didn't trust me, probably because of Emily. She had probably heard all about the debacle at the white chapel. I couldn't get a foot in the door with her, because my reputation had been ruined. She knew Emily's version of my narrative, and it was tainted. But trust, I knew, was also about lived experience, about the steps you take through pain with a person. I could still earn Gillian's trust.

Yet I knew as I sat with my sister that day in the car that as much as I wanted to save her, the price I would pay by empathizing with her was too great for me. There were spaces she lived to which I didn't want to follow her. I didn't want to see her life, my mother's daily deterioration. So I tried to insert Jesus, my solution to everything, the one who would take all the pain away. I tried to show her the benefits of my vantage point. She could be like me. She could accept Jesus and escape our earthly family, too. She could find herself in a land that was so much bigger than our mother, our childhood, our damage.

*

"Beth. These people *want* to hang out with you," Cate said from the couch across from me. Her perpetual teaching spot.

"I know," I said. "But I'm not sure they're good people."

"What do you mean? None of us are good people. That's why we need Jesus."

The people in question were the popular theater students. I had come to understand, since entering college, that hierarchies form in all places, and the college theater department was no exception. The best-looking people who got all the lead roles had, predictably, formed a clique. They hung out after rehearsal, ordered delivery at midnight, and posted pictures of their antics—cuddling in twin dorm beds, drinking unidentified liquids out of plastic cups.

And, suddenly, they were texting me. They were asking me to join in.

I didn't know what had prompted such an invitation. I felt no cooler than I had in high school, and I wasn't earning lead roles in any of the productions. It was a sore subject; I'd get called back to audition for those roles and then ultimately be cast as the eighty-year-old maidservant with one line. Every time a cast list came out, I'd spend at least a day crying, and Cate would make cupcakes and put on *Arrested Development*. "This is a chance to show people Jesus," she'd say after I calmed down enough to listen. "To be grateful with even the little you have and make them wonder how you're doing it."

Her direction was not much different when it came to these sudden invitations to spend time with the popular theater students. "Jesus is working. He's calling them to hang out with you, and you have this incredible opportunity to introduce people with *actual influence* to him."

It was a tendency I had not recognized yet inside of myself, this snobbery for people who were of a higher social stature than I was. Sure, I had once wanted to *be* one of them, but now I assumed they were all shallow, stabbing each other's backs in their ascent to the top.

"What are you scared of?" Cate asked.

"That they'll decide they hate me and then make my life miserable."

"Who cares if they do? God will protect you if that happens."

I thought of a time when I'd seen Cate drinking beer when we were studying abroad in England, where the drinking age was eighteen. A hard sight for me: my best friend, a Christian, partaking of a drink that I thought of as evil. "It's legal over here," she reminded me. "It's not bad, it's just normal." *Normal* was the word. Act, look, be normal. I had always been weird, but Christ was calling me to be normal, or at least to *seem* normal enough that people would be drawn to me and, in turn, to him.

Was my understanding obscured here, the essence of God's calling too complex for my good-and-evil-oriented mind? What if what I thought of as danger was really opportunity? Maybe people who drank alcohol weren't really evil, and maybe popular people were just future Jesus followers. Maybe the way I looked at the world needed to change in Christ's name. Maybe my field of consideration needed to widen so I could view the social elite around me the way that Jesus saw them—as sad, depraved souls that still needed saving.

But was the evangelical world really widening my vistas, or was it merely redirecting my attention? I had been recruited with the hope of God working wonders in my family, spiritually evolving them, growing them past their dysfunction. Now Cate was pointing outward, away from them. *Stop looking at your family. Look at the rest of the world.* As if saving my family had been secondary all along.

✷

One summer break, I was at the wheel of my parents' minivan. Emily sat in the passenger seat, and my mother sat in the row of seats behind us. Hoobastank's "The Reason" came on, and we listened as the singer musically informed us that his romantic relationship had made him a better person.

Disgust curdled at the back of my throat. "I hate this song," I said. "People don't change people."

My statement was meant for both sets of ears in the car. I

wanted my mother and sister to know the truth: that a person couldn't change for another person. God was the only one who could truly change someone's heart.

"I don't agree," Emily said.

"Doesn't matter if you agree or not," I said. "It's true."

"I think someone can inspire another person to change."

"But it won't be lasting change."

"How do you know?"

"Because feelings for people are fleeting and momentary," I said. "God is the only one that sticks."

"You don't know that."

Emily's doubt unleashed a torrent of passion in me that felt like rage. Why didn't she understand? Why was she resisting God's reality? I was angry that she, of all people, suffering from a terminal illness, refused to acknowledge the true nature of God—and the true nature of her disease. I knew what she'd been doing. She wasn't taking all of her medication, to see how she'd do without it. She had admitted to me once that she wasn't sure she really had cystic fibrosis. I worried that this stupid questioning would take her life sooner rather than later.

My voice raised, I told her that I *did* actually know that, because God had changed me for good and I could now see the falsehoods of manmade society. A person, I told her, was fallible and filled with idiosyncrasies, untrustworthy from day to day, a treacherous place to put your hope. Jesus was the only constant, the only way for us to find heaven—not just heaven at death but heaven in ourselves even through the mire of our sin. Only Jesus could change us into the people we were made to be.

"Jesus isn't the only way," she said. "I don't believe that."

"You're believing lies, then," I told her. "The truth isn't yours to decide."

She turned to the window so I wouldn't see her start to cry.

Cate would be proud. I stood by the truth. I didn't cave.

I parroted perfectly what she would have wanted me to say, with all the vigor and strength she would have brought to the conversation herself.

My mother, who had been silent the whole time, reached out from the back seat and touched Emily's arm. Her compassion annoyed me, and I wished she hadn't been there. With that touch, she made me feel like a bad guy, a sadist, because Emily's tears brought me a strange sense of joy. All I had done was drive a stake into the ground, similar to the one that Michelle, my Campus Crusade discipler, had driven for me early in my faith. Belief in Jesus Christ as Lord and Savior was the only way to heaven.

What I understood to be the truth solidified inside of me, even though it felt offensive and wrong. The whole world felt wrong, so why wouldn't the truth feel that way, too? It was a world that allowed entire villages to wash away in tsunamis, that enabled hurricanes to tear homes apart and drown impoverished babies. A world that gave four children to a mother who was so ravaged by her pain that she turned to prescription pills and threatened suicide to gain control over them. And that same mother was now offering my sister a compassion that I didn't feel she was qualified to give. What could redeem that type of conflict, that type of pain inside my head? Only a truth that was harsher than the world itself: There is no way to heaven other than belief in Jesus.

It was a belief that allowed for no perspective other than my own. I couldn't give credence to other ideas about finding salvation, or other methods to achieving happiness. I couldn't acknowledge Emily's grief. All I could see was Cate and Campus Crusade. I could no longer be with the very people I thought I was trying to save.

✷

There were some ways Cate couldn't change my point of view, even though she wanted to. One of my greatest burdens at the time was that I couldn't change it, either.

"You don't think being gay is a sin, do you?" I asked within my first month of converting.

"What do you think about it?" she asked.

"I've always thought it's okay."

"Why do you ask, then?"

"Because I know that some Christians don't."

Common knowledge from my liberal upbringing stated that while being gay was just as valid as being straight, there were Bible-thumping Christians who didn't see it the same way. My mother, a firm supporter of gay rights, who hung out with a lot of gay men in her nursing-school days, had warned me about such Christians. She said they were bigoted. I wanted to know what kind of Christians Cate and I were.

Cate told me that the Bible was a mysterious, God-breathed text, filled with all types of aphorisms and passages that were open to interpretation. However, there were some passages that needed no speculation, subjects that God was completely transparent about when he wrote the Bible through the souls of forty men. One of those subjects was homosexuality.

"The Bible is clear," Cate said, a phrase that I heard often throughout my time in the movement. "The act of homosexuality is a sin."

As the saying goes, it was a hard pill to swallow, and I'm not sure I ever made it go down. I hadn't admitted to myself yet that I was bisexual, that I found both men and women attractive since my earliest memories. (First crush: Michael J. Fox. Second crush: my babysitter, Pamela.) But I did have gay friends, and I was protective of them, of their right to love who they loved and have normal relationships.

In the face of Cate's Bible expertise, though, it was growing increasingly difficult to argue. "Why does God feel that way?" I asked.

"Because it's not in line with the way he created us. That means it's unnatural."

"But it doesn't hurt anybody."

"You don't know that. When we go out of God's order, it screws up our souls."

Her rationale was a brand of God logic I would soon become accustomed to, the kind that got away with claiming ultimate, superior truth without solid human reasoning because it came from someplace superhuman. You could throw an egg at this logic, watch the egg splatter, and then claim that maybe it was still intact, because who knew what *really* happened to the egg? Only God! Your eyes could be lying to you.

The only thing that would tell us the answers to our questions, even if they were answers that we didn't understand, was the Bible. The Bible would tell us if the egg cracked or bounced. When it came to homosexuality, I swore I saw it crack, because I couldn't think of a single thing that would make it bad for a person's soul. But now I was tasked with seeing it differently. I had to believe it bounced, because God said it did in the Bible.

So I walked through the world with what felt like two different sets of eyes: one that saw what it had always seen, and one that saw what God told it to see. When I asked Cate why I couldn't fully believe it, why I struggled with thinking that the act of homosexuality was a sin, she told me that it would take time for God to change my heart—time for him to take over and make me see what he saw. It was time for me to surrender what I *wanted* to be true in exchange for what *was* true, what he ordained to be true at the world's creation.

I learned many such illusions in Campus Crusade, but I inherited some from my childhood, too. I can now see a connection between the form of reality I gave in to during my time in the evangelical Christian movement and the form of reality my mother espoused with the pills she refused to stop taking. "These aren't hurting me," she told us as we watched the egg splatter. "I'm fine." The yolk slid down the wall. "I'm healthy." It hit the ground.

There are few greater pains than watching someone you love slowly kill themselves. It was a grief so large, so swallowing, that I chose instead the grief that came with following evangelical Jesus. "My burden is light," he said in Matthew 11:30, and I found it to be true. I spent months away from home, away from the burden the rest of my family was shouldering. It was, strangely, so much easier to worry that the whole world was going to hell than to experience the loneliness of my mother's addiction, so much easier to stand in massive churches filled with other believers singing to God and pleading for thousands of souls with our hands in the air. There was more hope in those rooms than there was sitting in confusion with my sisters, trying to figure out what an intervention looked like for someone who refused to admit that anything was wrong.

I gave in to beliefs that didn't feel right because it felt even worse to see my life as it was without them. This was my version of medicating myself, closing my eyes, diverting my attention—and I had a whole church filled with accomplices who taught me how to do it, who did it alongside me.

8.

I am the type of person who has always had a cat. I grew up with those agile, ornery creatures around my home and, from my earliest memories, have always wanted them to love me.

But none of the cats from my childhood loved me with the unconditional zeal of my current cat, Libby. I don't know if I was really ready to care for a cat when Libby came into my life as a kitten, but somehow, she still imprinted on me, as evidenced by the way she'd "nurse" on all my clothes, leaving giant wet spots in my lap. Libby is ten now, and she favors me above all other people, toys, cats, and windowsill birds. From the moment I wake up in the morning to when I close my eyes at night, she stares at me with wide eyes, trying to assess how best she can fit into my arms. She is, as many have witnessed, desperate for my love, staking me out the moment I sit on the couch so she can curl up into a bread loaf on my chest.

In a way, I feel worshipped by her. She is in tune with all my movements. She yells incomprehensible cat things at me, getting attention when she wants it by crying at doors or walls or the air—her own little form of prayer. She wants me to notice her, and I want her to love me always.

This is why I felt so hurt when she slept on the living room recliner one recent night. She usually sleeps next to my bed in what I call her "sidecar," a fuzzy little cat hammock held up by two scratching posts. When I wake, her head pops up, and she climbs into bed and paws at my face. But that one fateful night, she abandoned me for the recliner. I didn't know what made the recliner so special. Was it cooler, plusher, cleaner? The question was ultimately futile, because I was jealous of a chair, and there's no way of soothing such a useless sadness. Still, that sadness reappears like the scent of burning in my mind any morning I wake up to find the sidecar empty. It is there when I feel like she loves something else more than she loves me.

This is what I think of when I remember what Campus Crusade taught me about God's jealous grip on my love and attention. Worshipping anything other than God will turn that thing into an idol, Michelle, my Cru discipler, taught me. This version of idolatry was a complicated thing to learn. My perception of what constituted worship had completely changed since becoming an evangelical Christian. I used to think that worship was a rare occurrence, a conscious and dedicated act like praying or bowing down to something. But according to evangelical Christianity, worship was far more common and, potentially, far more dangerous. There was a fine line between being *interested* in something and *worshipping* it.

Do you really like the Beatles? Do you own all their records? Do you read about them a lot on the internet and hear their songs in your head before you fall asleep at night? Well, you might be worshipping the Beatles. They may be taking the place of God in your heart, a spot reserved for his perfect, persistently present, loving being. The problem is that if anything other than God occupies that spot, it won't be able to sustain your worship. It will disappoint you, fail to deliver on your needs, melt underneath the weight of your idolizing expectations. Eventually it will lead your soul to spontaneously combust from the inside.

Consequently, I was afraid of being too interested in anything, lest it become my new God and tear my spirit apart. I really liked acting, liked putting myself in the shoes of my characters, but I couldn't like it too much or else I'd lose myself in those characters—lose my way to the flame of Christ inside of me. I loved to sing, even felt that it was a form of worship, but I couldn't love it too much or else I'd sing myself out of communion with him, my focus flying from him toward the strength of my own voice. I loved to spend time with friends, to dig into our deepest feelings over hot cocoa or mint tea. I loved to discover what made people happy, what brought that swell of warmth into their days, whether it be wool socks or bright flowers or secretly keeping a ferret as a pet in their dorm. I loved to share those moments with them and build upon my own happiness, learning what it meant through their eyes and making it a part of my life.

But I now learned to feel guilty if those moments didn't include God, if I didn't invite him in to share those spaces with us. If I allowed myself to have a comfort that didn't hold some part of him, I was rejecting him, ignoring him, and degrading my own soul. If I liked even an egg sandwich a little too much, I could be worshipping it, so I protected my meals from idolatry by thanking God for the food on my plate.

When I learned about idols, about God's desire to be at the forefront of my mind, I understood what I was being taught: that he was the only one I could really rely on. But on an emotional level, I internalized something deeper than that. I saw pieces of myself in his insistence at being present, his own need to be known, to be in on the moment. I sympathized with him, this poor jealous creature, who only wanted to be a part of my every move. I knew what it was like to be left out, and I didn't want to do that to the lover of my soul.

✷

One of my very first idols, I've come to realize, was a daycare provider named Mrs. Campbell. From the ages of two months to five years, I attended her daycare with my brother while our parents worked. She was a large, sharp-keyed perm addict who walked with a heavy gait. Most mornings, my father dropped my brother and me off at Mrs. Campbell's, ushering us into a living room where about ten other children played. She would hug us and speak sweetly to us, until our father walked out the door. Then she'd look through us like we didn't exist, pushing past us into the kitchen to read her magazines.

I had a need to be liked when I was a child, a need to get confirmation that I was a good person, a good kid. I needed adults to tell me that I was good at doing cartwheels, that the cookies I baked with my mom were delicious. I wanted to be someone's favorite, because I thought that meant I was worth something, that I'd grow up to do good things and be a worthwhile person. As a teenager, this became a hopeless devotion to the pursuit of popularity, an idolization of the girls in school who seemed like they were going somewhere. But before that, when I was a small child, Mrs. Campbell was the one I wanted to impress.

I wasn't one of Mrs. Campbell's favorites, and I knew that was because I often got in trouble. When you got in trouble, bad things happened. I remember sitting in a high chair, three years old, not wanting to eat the macaroni and cheese she'd made because it was shell shaped and I preferred tubes. She began stuffing them in my mouth as I struggled, coughing, almost choking. That was the way she treated all the children who weren't her favorites. When a child misbehaved, she dragged them into the kitchen, pulled down their pants, and spanked them bare-bottom. The sound of their cries was a warning. I didn't want that to happen to me, so I tried to be perfect and do nothing wrong and blend in with the good kids.

One day, when I was at her house by myself, I drew her a

picture. I brought it from the living room into the kitchen, where she was sitting at the kitchen table.

"This is nice," she said, taking it from my hands. "Thank you." She reached over and hugged—actually *hugged*—me.

I was elated. I couldn't believe she liked it. At last I had found the key to her favor! I went back to the living room and drew another picture, quickly. She needed it, I needed it, I wanted her to like me, I wanted to survive. I finished and brought the second picture to the kitchen, where she was concentrating on something that involved a checkbook and a calculator.

I tapped her shoulder and presented the drawing to her.

She glanced at it briefly. "Thanks," she said, then looked back at the task in front of her.

I was disappointed. Maybe this picture wasn't as good. What was it about that first one that had made her so grateful? I sat down again and again and tried to replicate that first reaction. I used the brightest colors and drew the biggest shapes. I hoped I could win her favor back, but it seemed to slip away a little more each time I brought her a picture. Her voice got deeper, her face angrier.

"Stop!" she finally said, and I knew it was over. I had ruined it, and I would never get that first reaction back.

According to the logic of evangelical Christianity, Mrs. Campbell had become an idol for me. Even though I feared her, I also revered her and needed her affirmation. I saw my worth through her eyes. It was an insubstantial worth, but it was worth nonetheless. It was a representation of how the world saw me, and it was something I hoped to change. This was, I learned, a perspective that grieved God—little me seeking approval from someone other than him. "Let the children come to me," Jesus had said in Mark 10:14. "Do not hinder them, for to such belongs the kingdom of God."

In college, I came to understand idolatry as the great

problem of my childhood, deeper than the sins of my parents, the suicidality of my mother. It was my attachment to my caretakers, my need for their affection, that had done the deepest damage and disturbed the natural order of my development. I had not been taught how to rely on my creator and had instead been reaching into empty wells to discover the truth of who I was. Evangelicalism taught me that idolatry had left me alone, because my caretakers were not built to shoulder the burden of my affirmation—particularly since they were not believers themselves. And it was because of idolatry, I believed, that I was left vulnerable to their actions, that they were given the emotional power to hurt me in the first place.

One day, in the living room of Mrs. Campbell's daycare, a girl I was playing with called me stupid. She was a designated good kid with curly blond hair and a cooler name than mine: Tatiana. Mrs. Campbell never yelled at her and she never got in trouble. When she called me stupid that day, in the center of a circle of toys, I slapped her in the face.

The world went slow as I was wrenched into the kitchen by Mrs. Campbell. I heard the sound of my own cries as she turned me bottom-up in her lap and sent pain rushing through my body. When it was done, I sat in the kitchen corner until she told me I could leave.

As an evangelical, I often remembered the sadness of that moment, the sense of betrayal, the anger at myself for falling into the crossfire of Mrs. Campbell's rage. And I felt God comfort me, the small child who still lived inside, who was never meant to give all that affection to someone so volatile.

It was the greatest relief to believe that, in God, I had finally found someone to worship who would never break my heart.

✷

Cate was upset when I decided to audition for a production of Anton Chekhov's *The Seagull* that my friend was directing off campus. "You said that you were going to lead Bible study this semester," she said.

I didn't contradict her. I vaguely remembered agreeing to do it, plus Cate wasn't known to exaggerate or lie. She also wasn't known to get angry, or annoyed, or stirred to emotion by much of anything. She was generally stoic and reasonable beyond comprehension. This was new, this reaction.

"I just want to audition," I said. "I may not even get a part."

"Well, what if you do? Then I'll be leading by myself again."

"We may not have rehearsals on Wednesdays. I could still do it."

"With what energy? What'll you be able to bring to it?"

I couldn't answer. She had never questioned my energy before, my ability to multitask or deliver or do something well. I didn't really have an explanation beyond the fact that I was a theater major, I wanted to be an actor one day, and I had a right to audition for this play. But what rights did I really have? Campus Crusade had begun teaching me that I *didn't* have rights in the eyes of God. We had forfeited them at the fall, when Adam and Eve disobeyed God. I was entitled to nothing, not even the blessings God gave me freely.

Cate was silent for a moment, calculating her response. I could tell she was parsing her words. "When is this going to stop?" she finally said. "When are you going to start putting God first?" She then brought up the tears I shed every audition season, my inconsolable sadness at not being cast in lead roles, how I seemed to hinge my life on those productions. She also brought up my lack of involvement in our local church, how I had yet to really experience what it was like to be a part of a biblical body of believers.

"I'm involved in Cru," I said, defending myself.

"But that's not church!" she said. "Cru's a college ministry. You need to get plugged in at a church."

I told her I didn't have time. She told me I needed to make time. She asked what I was going to do if I became an actor, if I was touring around the country and not going to church on Sundays. I told her that I would do daily devotionals on my own. She told me that wasn't enough. I needed a church community.

Every sign seemed to indicate she was disappointed in me, that she thought I was screwing up my life. She was angry at my decisions, an anger I hadn't been aware of, that hadn't burst until now. "I'm hurt by you," she said. "I'm hurt that you don't devote yourself to this ministry."

I got the message: I needed to be doing more. I was attending classes all day and rehearsing for shows all night. I thought I had been doing my best, but my best simply wasn't good enough. In Cate's eyes, I was drowning in idolatry, for the shows I acted in and the people I acted beside and the major I wanted to make into a profession. I was putting that first, putting too much emotion into it, placing it above God and caring more about these roles than I was caring about him.

Did God feel the same? Did he see my actions in the same light? Did he feel pushed aside, slighted by my adoration of the art? I had not thought so until that moment, had not felt the pang of his sadness until Cate admonished me.

But was it his sadness? Or was it Cate's?

Was Cate, in fact, my idol?

If I was idolizing Cate, I wasn't the only one. I think she was an idol to all the women who were a part of our Cru ministry—a ministry that was as much a club as it was a generalized group of friends. Our tribe had a hierarchy that couldn't be denied, even though we didn't talk about it and pretended it wasn't there. Cate sat in the back of our thoughts, in a place that was supposed to house Jesus, and she stayed present behind our conversations, guiding our actions in her absence. When we had doubts about our decisions, about our feelings and thought processes, we genuinely wanted to know: What would Cate do? What would Cate say?

When we didn't have her to talk to, we tried to be like her. I remember talking on the phone with Hannah, our vice president, about a guy I had a crush on—a punk with dark hair that he wore in spikes, a Green Day bumper sticker on the back of his car. He was not a Christian, so he was forbidden, and on top of it all, had a girlfriend. "Tell him you're a Christian and you're abstinent," said Hannah. "Then he'll stop flirting and go away!" She herself struggled deeply with waiting until marriage. Any time she "slipped up" sexually and "did something inappropriate with a guy," she'd confess it to Cate, who would then tell me how it grieved her that Hannah had already done so much. "I wish I talked about my abstinence more," Hannah said that day over the phone. "It seems easier for Cate. I wish I was as strong as her."

We all did, and Cate knew it. It was not something she necessarily discouraged. As a pastor's child, she had learned to set positive examples, to show us perspectives we too could achieve if we prayed to God for them. The rest of us struggled with feeling beautiful after being told we were ugly in high school, but Cate didn't. No matter who a bully was, she didn't internalize a word they said. The rest of us struggled with the fear that we'd never have sex because we'd never find a Christian man who'd love us enough to marry us, but Cate didn't. She trusted God so completely that she had actually dumped a good Christian man because, she claimed, God told her to free her mind before a mission trip overseas. No matter the cost, she abided in him.

Be more like Christ, be more like me, was the message we got from Cate. She was glad that we wanted to be like her, as long as we revered her in the way she wanted us to.

✷

What evangelical Christianity taught me about idols rang true, because I had been hurt by people I wanted to find myself in. I'd experienced the disappointment, the outside-in explosion, the pain that comes from needing something that a person can never give you. There had been adults who broke a trust I instinctually gave them, a trust to protect me, to grow me, to make me into a full person.

When Cate informed me I was idolizing theater, the words were like a bell, and I had to decide whether or not to listen.

At first, I didn't. I auditioned for *The Seagull* anyway. I was cast as Irina Arkadina, a role I was eager to play, and threw myself into her character at rehearsal three nights a week. The director decided to take some liberties with the stage directions and said that Irina and her boyfriend, Boris Trigorin, should be making out throughout most of the opening scenes. I did as the director asked and kissed the hell out of Boris, who was played by my gay friend Bill, until I began going home full of sinful thoughts. I would climb into bed and close my eyes and imagine the kissing going further, imagine Bill bursting into my dorm, yelling "I'm not gay!" and climbing into my bed for a night of raucous sex.

The whole time, a distance grew between Cate and me. She contacted me less, asked me to join her at fewer meals, and, I believed, trusted me less. I led only one Bible study that whole semester, and I felt shame for that.

When the play was over and we took our final bows, I was so guilty about the sexual fantasies and about my absence from Bible study that I regretted the entire production. I regretted not listening to Cate. I decided to own a new perspective: she had been right all along. I shouldn't have auditioned.

I told Cate about my new perspective after the last Cru meeting of the semester, when we were putting the Bibles into boxes.

"Okay," she said. "I forgive you." And I felt the distance close.

✷

Despite the pain it caused me, despite my inability to admit it to myself, Cate was my idol. But I was also loved by her. I knew this because she said so in a Christmas card she wrote to me over winter break. It was dark blue with the image of a starry night sky, snowflakes falling on a cozy-looking house with smoke coming out of the chimney. Inside, she wrote a long note in pink pen. She let me know how proud she was for every leap of faith I had taken. She said that listening to me pray led her closer to God. She felt blessed through me on a daily basis. *I don't say it or show it nearly enough,* she wrote, *but I. Love. You.* In my complicated way, I loved her too.

That same winter break, she called me and let me know that she had gotten drunk for the first time. She'd just turned twenty-one and her nonbelieving high school friends had taken her out for her birthday. She had a drink at dinner, and then another at one of their houses, and eventually so many that she felt glued to the couch, legs too gelatinous to hold her body. She learned that she was a chatty drunk, as she spent the whole night talking to people on the couch as if they had just entered her office.

Hearing her tell the story, a double-standard alert went off hard in my head. Our faith didn't prohibit us from consuming alcohol, but the Bible was clear in Ephesians 5:18 about its stance on drunkenness: "And do not get drunk with wine, for that is debauchery." Cate was admitting sin to me, but it sounded like she was telling me a story about something fun she had done that weekend.

"So," she said after finishing. She was silent, waiting for me to respond.

"Sounds like quite the experience," I said.

"Yeah," she said. "But it was wrong. You can say that." She told me that she needed me to speak truth to her, to call her out on her sin, to hold her accountable to God in this way. "I know you're not happy about this. I need to hear that."

I wasn't happy, she was correct. I felt disappointed and hurt, as if my parents had forgotten to pick me up at school. Why was she asking me to call her out on a sin that she *knew* was a sin? Was she not convinced that she had sinned? Was Cate, my expert on holiness, confused about the definition of sin? How could my role model—my idol—do something wrong? There was anger and there was confusion, but there was also a person on the line, a person waiting for me to speak, to hear the fullness of my reaction.

I asked the question. "Did it feel like you were sinning?"

"No," she said. "That's what's so weird. It felt normal."

I put my Cate hat on, the same one I always tried to use on myself, and told her what I knew she would have said to me. "Our feelings can't be trusted. The Bible is clear on this matter."

"I know," she said. "I need to hear that."

I wondered if my idol suffered from not having an idol of her own, from not having someone tangible to hang the weight of her faith on. I wondered if she suffered from providing that kind of support to so many people but having to rely on an invisible God to do the same for her. We weren't supposed to put her in that position, but we did, and she took it on, perhaps because it made her feel powerful or good, or perhaps because she didn't know what else to do. Maybe she wanted us to know Jesus because it would help her know Jesus. Our faith would give her the courage and hope she needed, too.

✷

My cat Libby sits in my lap, her body between me and my keyboard. She cleans herself as I type at a distance. She places herself in a position of top priority, the place my laptop was in before she sat down and pushed it aside. I let her do this, most of the time. I know I will not always have this. Her idolization of me is lovely but transient, as fleeting as all of us. "Our life is a blink," Cate used to say. What a beautiful blink it is with Libby here.

For so long, I made a conscious effort not to trust my idols. Cate and I acknowledged them out loud and put up barriers against them. I had to prioritize; I had to put God first. But there was also an unacknowledged idol, Cate, and I didn't know how to put a barrier between her and myself. She was a part of my mind. I saw the world through her eyes. She was an idol I thought I needed, who had put herself in that position. I still find myself wanting to be logical like her—wanting to break through all feeling to a place where I can rest.

But the idols of our childhood often beget the idols of our adulthood, and I can't help but see the connection between Mrs. Campbell and Cate. With both of them, I felt a need to be seen favorably by people who represented power—the power over others that came with leading a daycare or a ministry, the power over oneself that came from pragmatism and confidence. It was all wrapped up with abuse, from hands and from words, but I can see now that when it came to Cate, the abuse was familiar. It was the kind of abuse I had grown up with, so kindred I didn't see it as foreign. When I didn't do what she wanted, she distanced herself from my life. The threat of losing her presence, like the threat of losing my mother, was what urged me to action. I wonder now if the manipulation gave me a sense of comfort.

In the midst of this sat a version of God who was aggrieved, who was watching me find my ultimate joy, my ultimate worth, in opinions other than his own. And I think now that the greatest abuser of all is the one who makes it impossible for his children to survive in the world he has built for them, by causing them to cosmically combust when they don't give him the attention he claims to deserve. I had given my heart to a being who had created it to be broken, because I would never find happiness without personal autonomy. I would never find freedom in the cage I was told he created for us.

9.

The setting: senior year of high school. The scene: a heated student council debate. I stood with my notes on top of a small bookcase, towering above the people seated around me. I had somehow become the vice president of the student council the year before, winning the election by a mere two votes. Morgan, sitting at one of the tables below me, held the title of "state liaison," which meant that she got to skip school to go to conferences.

As a council, we were planning the upcoming Spirit Week, but couldn't agree on what event to conduct on Thursday—a scavenger hunt or a talent show. Morgan and I were advocating for the talent show. "Everyone at this school thinks they're the next big thing," Morgan said when it was her turn to talk. "Why aren't we putting on a talent show?"

Hailey, a popular junior, took the floor. "A scavenger hunt would be fun. We could hide eggs around the school."

I used my vice-presidential powers to interject. "Scavenger hunts are for babies. We're almost adults."

"No one's going to come to a talent show," Mrs. Waggoner, one of the two faculty advisers for student council, interjected.

"That's right," agreed Mrs. Milton, the other faculty adviser. "Plus, no one will want to come to school after school hours."

Morgan and I thought it was unbelievable that during the

extremely admired second season of *American Idol*, when the whole country was fighting over whether Ruben Studdard or Clay Aiken was the better singer, we were getting pushback about putting on a talent show. We chalked it up to the advisers siding with the popular kids over us. We decided to talk to them privately.

At lunch, we went into Mrs. Milton's office, a windowless room with a small round table where she and Mrs. Waggoner ate, and cut them a deal. "Let us put on a talent show," we said. "We'll front the money. If it's a flop, we'll eat the funds. If it's packed, we'll reimburse ourselves and give the council the rest of the money."

"Do what you want!" Mrs. Milton said. "Just don't expect the school to pay you back if you fail!"

✷

Morgan and I came up with a plan of action. First, we spread out a long roll of paper until it was taller than any of us. Then we wrote "SOUTHBRIDGE IDOL! TALENT SHOW! APRIL 21! SIGN UP IN THE LIBRARY!" on the paper and pasted it to the hallway outside the principal's office, covered in glitter. We also announced the upcoming talent show over the intercom every morning, after the English/Spanish pledge of allegiance. Within a week, we had fifteen acts signed up to compete. We gave them each a four-minute slot, convinced some teachers to act as judges (thinking intricately about who was equivalent to Randy, Simon, and Paula), and held a dress rehearsal. We even made sashes for the first and second place winners.

The night of the show, there wasn't an empty seat in the auditorium. Students came. Parents came. People were so eager to be there they sat in the aisles. The night was a smashing success.

At the end of the show, as Morgan and I were cleaning up, Mrs. Waggoner and Mrs. Milton had nothing but words of praise for us. "Bethorgan" they called us, amalgamating our names.

"Moreth! You are an incredible team!" As we drove home that night, we talked about how empty their praise felt. We wished they had believed in us and supported our efforts in the first place.

About a week later, an op-ed showed up in our local newspaper, the *Southbridge Evening News*. It was written by an anonymous person, and it was all about Southbridge Idol. The writer credited Mrs. Waggoner and Mrs. Milton for the show, saying they had brought the school together in a triumph of unity for the town.

Lava erupted from my ears. Who wrote this piece of trash? I would be damned if those treacherous teachers got credit for what we did!

I wrote an anonymous op-ed of my own, one that told the truth about who was behind Southbridge Idol. I not only provided the names of all the students who had helped us put on the show, I also exposed Mrs. Waggoner and Mrs. Milton for the way they ignored certain voices in the student council. Without mincing words, I compared them to dictators. I sent my manifesto via email to the *Southbridge Evening News* and immediately felt a sense of release. My anger had been quelled.

Three days later, I already regretted writing it. What if it got published? What would I do then? A week passed, and I thought I was home free. And then one more day passed. That's when Mrs. Milton came running down the hall calling Mrs. Waggoner's name in the middle of a class I had with her.

Mrs. Waggoner walked out of the room. "What?" she asked, sounding annoyed.

Mrs. Milton's voice shook. "Someone bashed us in the *Southbridge Evening News*."

I sat there in class as Mrs. Waggoner took the paper and read my words out loud to all twenty of us.

"Signed, Anonymous!" she read. "What a coward!"

I felt the blood dribble out of my face.

"Beth! Poor girl! You've gone white!" said Mrs. Waggoner.

"Don't worry, sweetheart," said Mrs. Milton. "We'll find out who wrote this."

I blurted out the only words that came to mind: "I don't know who would write something like that about you!"

"We need to keep this a secret for ten years minimum!" Morgan told me later. "My little brother will be done with high school by then."

After I became an evangelical, the story of my courageous letter to the *Southbridge Evening News* editor made me feel ashamed of the way I lied to Mrs. Waggoner and Mrs. Milton. My Christian friends would laugh through most of the story, but discomfort always brewed when we got to the lying part.

"I'm not proud of what I did," I'd say, my great caveat. "But I didn't know God back then."

Courage in the church was the opposite of what I had shown in Mrs. Waggoner's class. It wasn't shrinking away, denying your actions or beliefs. It was believing so fully that the belief spilled out of you, believing until there was no room for anything but belief.

Believing was telling the truth, which was another word for evangelism.

✷

"Summer Project" was Cru's term for a summer mission trip. Cate had attended one overseas during junior year. Now, in senior year, she urged me to sign up for one as well. She couldn't recommend the spiritual growth I would receive highly enough. "You need something if you're going to grow in your relationship with God after college," she said. Still feeling guilty about the way my appearing in *The Seagull* had distracted me from my faith, I applied for a Summer Project in Botswana, where Cru claimed the ground was spiritually fertile. It could be a fun, faith-building experience,

I thought, to spend the summer in another country, to see God work in ways Cate told me would solidify my faith forever.

I didn't get in to the Botswana trip, but the rejection email included a list of other Summer Projects that still had slots open. I hastily applied for the first one I saw—a ten-week trip to Hampton Beach, New Hampshire. Spending a summer in New Hampshire was not the most exhilarating prospect, but it was all I could think to do if I was going to prepare my soul for a life in New York City the following year, as I had been accepted into the master's program in creative writing at The New School. I heard Cate's voice in my head: *When is God going to come first?* I didn't want to disappoint her again.

However, there was a catch: in order to go to Hampton Beach, I had to raise $2,900 to fund my own trip. I called Cate immediately to ask her how on earth I was supposed to manage that. "Through prayer" was her response. Since she had left the country for her Summer Project, she'd had to raise even more, and she warned me about the spiritual and mental difficulties that came with relying on God for a large sum of money. She agreed to mentor me as I went through the process.

First thing was first: I needed to create a Facebook group.

"Seriously?" I said. "Can't I just write letters to Christian people?"

"No!" she answered. "This is missional in itself. You need to let nonbelievers know you're going on this trip and then share your testimony when they ask why."

Ambivalently, I set up a Facebook group titled "Beth's Going to Hampton Beach and She Needs YOUR Help!" I posted a support letter, based on a template from Cru, to do all the awkward explaining for me: *So, with graduation being about three weeks away, I'm writing to let you know about the exciting things that God is doing in my life and how I would LOVE for you to be a part of them! About four years ago, I became involved with Campus Crusade, drawn toward the life-values and genuine friendships that I witnessed among the members. I yearned to have friendships like that myself. A year and a half later, I entered into the greatest friendship of all, a personal relationship with Jesus Christ, and I have been mentored and built up in my faith by the loving staff and members of Campus Crusade ever since!*

The letter went on to explain what I would be doing on the trip, with many superfluous exclamation points, since I was supposed to be excited about it. Along with attending rigorous Bible study sessions, I would also be tasked with getting a job near so that I could share the gospel with my coworkers via the Knowing God Personally tract booklet. And, because Cru loved initiative evangelism, I'd also be involved in "outreaches" on the beach itself, approaching beachgoers and asking to sit on their blankets so they could participate in a quick spiritual survey.

In the final paragraph of the letter, through the words of Cru, I made my paramount plea: *In order to make all this possible, I need to develop a team of ministry partners—a group of people like you who would give to make my trip possible. As you might imagine, raising the necessary funds will be one of my greatest steps of faith in preparation for the summer. I need a total of $2,900 by May 31st, which covers room and board for the summer. Would you prayerfully consider joining my team by giving a gift of $25, $50, $100 or more? Whatever the Lord leads you to, even if it is less than that, is the right amount!*

I winced as I invited all my theater friends to join the group, and sent digital invitations to classmates and friends from home as well as distant family members. "It's a leap of faith," Cate said. It was courage that I was called to, so I tried to muster up the same bravery that had arisen within me when I skewered Mrs. Waggoner and Mrs. Milton in the *Southbridge Evening News.*

When I was younger, the idea of courage seemed internally transformative. Outwardly, I was a girl living in the early 2000s, when flared jeans were still trendy and people wore them low in a way that felt weird on my hips. I was generally uncomfortable in clothes and didn't know how to look the way I wanted: like a badass Jedi, a woman who could drown the antagonists of the world in elven spells. Courage could make me that type of person on the inside, at least. It could bestow upon me the powers that existed in my favorite stories.

Then Christianity came along and gave me a new view of courage, one based on the idea of "spiritual battle." According to the church, the spiritual realm existed around and inside of us. It was a place where demons fought angels for my thoughts, the birthplace of my struggles to feel worthy in the world. The spiritual realm was the reason I felt ugly even though I was created in God's image. It was the ground that demons won when a Christian cheated on their spouse, or had sex before marriage, or kept quiet about their faith in the workplace. It was the site of the battles that occurred within, and it tipped the scales of our belief, our self-esteem, our personality.

Having courage as a Christian meant becoming a warrior of that realm. It meant joining the angels, taking up a sword, turning into the inner heroine I had always wanted to be, and at last, experiencing the affirmation that came with entire churches full of people identifying me as such. Or so I told myself as I asked everyone I knew for money on Facebook.

✷

For my senior theater project, I wrote a play that was produced and performed in our university's black box theater. I titled it *Call Me Goliath*, and it contained "subversive," "biblical" themes. It was a dank, dreary tale of two brothers who lived together after their parents died in a car accident. The complex noir narrative involved vomit, bloodshed, and a taxidermied horse head, as well as other macabre devices that I used to create the most intense environment I could envision. I wanted my audiences to know that this was a serious story about serious things, such as humanity's inner demons and the sinful "Goliaths" that reside in our minds. If I could get people to acknowledge their wickedness, their spiritual sickness, then perhaps I could lead them to the soul doctor: Jesus Christ, Lord and Savior.

In order to do that, I had to figure out a way to mention him in the play. I was accustomed to talking about God in my program bios, thanking him for saving my soul and inspiring the directors to cast me in so-and-so play. But this was different: It was *my* play, *my* project. How could I take advantage of that for the Lord? How could I squeeze him in naturally, without embarrassing him or myself?

Tara, who had been president of our Cru chapter when she was a student, had recently joined Cru's professional staff and was back on campus all the time, like a Christian-lady version of Van Wilder. Michelle, the discipler who had corrected my wrongheaded notion that Jesus wasn't the only way to heaven, had left her job to raise children, and Tara was her replacement.

Tara began texting me about discipling sessions, but I wasn't sure about her ability to spiritually lead me. I had always sensed insincerity in her perky personality, something that felt *off* in her copious smiley-face text messages. Regardless, she was my sister in Christ, and Cate told me that he could work through our personality differences.

For our first discipling session, we went to Arby's and discussed my play over chicken sandwiches and curly fries.

"You *have* to acknowledge Jesus," Tara said. "He's the reason you even got this opportunity."

"I know. I want to, I just don't know when."

"Well, will you have a chance to address the audience?"

"Yes. We're doing a talkback."

"How much will you be talking?"

"I don't know? I guess a lot."

Tara suggested I share the gospel during the talkback, which was not the response I wanted.

"That sounds great," I said. "But I don't know how to make it seem natural."

"Natural? What do you mean?"

"To do it in a way where I represent God well." I didn't want to represent the Jesus I knew and loved as someone associated with anything other than goodness, and I didn't want to look like a Bible-thumping crazy person. I didn't want to watch the theater empty out like it had for the Christian magician.

"I know it's scary," Tara said. "And I know that this isn't what you want to hear, but you have to die to yourself. Let God take over. Have courage."

Courage. There was that word again, that word of transformation. Here it was in the context of something that could humiliate me, words that could pour out of my mouth and make me into a pariah. Did I have the courage to be cast out for something I believed? To be metaphorically slain for loving Jesus, for being convinced that he was the world's sole savior? If it turned me into the warrior that I always wanted to be, could I find the strength to let it in? Was this the type of thing that people risked for God?

Yes, was the answer. At least, that's what the Bible seemed to say. People put themselves on the line for God all the time, risking things as serious, as final, as death. In the biblical book named for her, Esther risked her life by bravely entering the king's court and asking him to save the Jewish people from death. In Luke 8:3, Joanna risked her entire livelihood by supporting Jesus in his ministry, even though her husband was King Herod's household manager. So many stories were about people dying to themselves, to the people they once wanted to be, because they obeyed God so wholeheartedly.

Why should I be any different? I wanted to take up my cross in the line of warriors, in the royal priesthood of the faithful who found their worth in God because they didn't see it anywhere else.

✷

I have a plan to help you raise money for your trip, the text message said.

It was from Alicia, a friend from the theater department. She had a massive, dazzling smile and somehow went to class, worked a job, attended daily play rehearsals, and organized boisterous parties in her dorm. She felt like my opposite in many ways, a young woman fully immersed in the secular. Yet she loved me, even though I was nothing like her.

I met her one evening outside of our dorm building, and we walked to the cafeteria together.

"There's cupcake mix and frosting on sale at Shoprite," she said. "What if I buy you twenty boxes and we sell the cupcakes at the show for a dollar?"

Alicia was so resourceful.

We went to the Shoprite and filled two handheld baskets with cupcake mix and frosting, strategizing the bake sale as we dumped the boxes on a conveyor belt. I confirmed with the heads of the theater department that selling cheap baked goods outside of the auditorium was acceptable, and Alicia scheduled people to oversee the table, since I would be in the play. In the end, we sold every cupcake, bringing in $240 for my trip.

Later, after the play was over and I was making spaghetti in my dorm, there was a knock at the door. I opened it to find Sarah, who had been in the play with me, standing there with her arms around a heavy-looking plastic jar.

"I have something for you. Wanna see?"

Sarah lugged the jar into my room and placed it on the table, shaking her arms out with a big grin.

"What do we have here?" I asked.

"It's a jar I've been putting change in since I was a kid. I counted it today. Over seventy dollars."

I stared at the jar and tried to calculate how many quarters were inside it.

"I want you to have it! For your trip."

The support that came from my nonbelieving friends made up over 60 percent of all my donations. They skimmed money off the top of their nearly empty bank accounts and gave me their final work-study paychecks for the semester. I had a hard time accepting that it was really happening, that they were rallying together so much for me, for a cause I knew they didn't fully understand. But that didn't seem to matter. It just mattered that it was for me.

"God's being faithful to you," Cate said when I told her, and it was hard not to see it that way.

✷

Two weeks before the school year ended, I received a message from Jack, an acquaintance I had invited to my Facebook group. He wrote that he would be happy to give me some money for my trip, but since he was an advocate for marriage equality, he wanted to know if Cru was affiliated with a conservative or a liberal church, and what the group's stance was on the issue.

I knew exactly what Campus Crusade's stance was on marriage equality, and it was not the type of thing I wanted to discuss with a nonbeliever, much less a gay rights activist.

I immediately texted Cate: *EMERGENCY!*

She called a staff member to get guidance on the situation, and then suggested that I write Jack back and tell him that Cru was a nondenominational ministry with no church affiliation, but that I'd be open to grabbing coffee and discussing the issue further.

"But we do have the same beliefs as many churches," I said.

"Sure, but we're not directly affiliated with any of them. We don't call them 'Campus Crusade–approved churches.'"

"But we're taught that homosexuality is a sin."

"But we're not a Republican organization. We don't *tell people* to be Republican."

I wrote Jack back: *Campus Crusade isn't affiliated with any single church or any ONE denomination of Christianity, nor is it affiliated with political stances or political parties. But if you'd like to know more about Cru's stance on all this jazz, we could totally get together for coffee sometime. :-)*

I knew I was being intentionally cryptic, but there was nothing about what I wrote that wasn't the truth. Still, it felt like I was sidestepping the issue. In this case, Cru didn't tell me to be courageous, didn't tell me to stand up for what I believed. They told me, instead, to try and avoid the conversation.

But did I really believe that the act of homosexuality was a sin? If I did, wouldn't I have felt different? Wouldn't I have wanted to have the conversation, no matter how unpopular it made me? No matter the risk?

That was the person I had been, but it wasn't the person I was becoming. I thought it had to be because of Satan. He was making me scared.

✷

Call Me Goliath ran to a full audience. I sat in the lighting booth and watched my vision unfurl on the stage. In the sordid world I'd created, the actors kissed and cried in the depravity of their mortal souls. The audience, I could see, was captivated. Something about what I had written resonated. This was no Kirk Cameron's *Fireproof*. They did not realize they were watching an evangelical Christian play.

As the show ended and my friends began to take their bows, I prayed about the talkback. *God, help me glorify you with my words.*

Help me show them the real you. I imagined myself stammering, tripping over offenses, caught in desperation as I tried to maintain God's image. Was it his image, or mine? Or were our images now entwined?

On my cue, I leapt onto the stage, took a bow of my own, and swirled around to see my parents in the audience. Cate and Tara were behind them, sitting together, cheering. There was no turning back now. I had a responsibility to all these souls, and I knew that Cate and Tara were there to hold me to it.

The stagehands set up a row of chairs behind us, and I sat between the actors, who were still in costume as we prepared for audience questions. The first few people to raise their hands asked the actors about "in-character" experiences, but it didn't take long for someone to direct a question to me.

"How did you come up with this?" a woman in the back asked. "And what is the main message you hope to get across?"

There it was. The perfect opportunity to talk about God from heaven above.

"Well, my faith encompasses everything I do," I said. "I'm a Christian, and I wrote this play to explore the concept of biblical separation from God." I proceeded to talk about original sin and how I believed it affected us. I explained that "sin" meant "missing the mark," like in archery. This play imagined a ripple effect created by a series of mistakes, which ultimately resulted in chaos—turning the world grim instead of bright. "Obviously, this is all in a pre-redemption context. There's no Jesus to save the characters in this play. There's just the monsters we all have to face inside of ourselves."

Heads nodded in the audience. I had gotten my point across.

After the talkback was over, I found Tara and Cate.

"You did wonderful!" Tara squealed, arms wrapping around my neck. "You shared the whole gospel!"

I hadn't, but Tara was prone to exaggeration. I looked at Cate while I was caught in Tara's headlock, and she smiled earnestly, close-lipped, her eyes telling me she was proud.

"You did good," she said.

That night, on the verge of sleep, I wondered if I had done enough, if Cate and Tara were praising me like a parent who's been given a poorly drawn handprint turkey by their child. Did it *really* look like a turkey, or did it look like I couldn't trace? Had I effectively planted seeds, or had I gone over people's heads?

It was my lack of courage that kept me from stating, definitively, that Jesus Christ was Lord. It was my fear of rejection, of failure, that left my tract booklets at home. The part of me that felt like I was just beginning to get cool, just beginning to seem normal, kept me from shouting God's name from the theater rooftop. It was my own sin, I decided. It was the monster inside of myself. God was blessing me with respect and notoriety, and I didn't want to give that up for him. I wasn't brave enough.

But we had to be brave, because God's message was, in many ways, offensive. It was otherworldly, non-human, beyond what we could understand. We were made in God's image but we were far from being like him, far from the omnipotence and sinlessness that explained his goodness even when, say, an entire village perished in a tsunami. Abraham did not question God when he was told to sacrifice his own son, because he knew that what felt wrong to him could be right in the eyes of God. He knew that sin had polluted his human mind away from true understanding. It grieved him, but he brought Isaac up that mountain because he trusted God to always be good, to only do good even if it killed the person he loved most in the world. Or so I was taught by evangelical Christianity.

✸

I never got back to Jack about meeting up for coffee. He responded to my message, but I couldn't imagine telling a gay man that he was an abomination.

At the end of the school year, as I packed my belongings, I remembered Cate's logic workaround, the way she told me to step aside. *We're not a Republican organization. We don't tell people to be Republican.* I knew what it felt like when I truly believed in something, when something stirred me so much that I could write an enraged letter to the editor about it. But the church told me that feeling had to disappear if I was going to follow God. My senses were warped, my understanding off-kilter, my heart too sinful to understand what God deemed sin.

And so, along with my belongings, I packed up my pride. I packed up the idea that I had a right to understand. I needed Cru's Summer Project to renew my faith.

10.

When I first learned what sex was as a seven-year-old (after asking my mother about it in front of a school crossing guard), I was so disgusted that I inquired about other options for pregnancy. My mother said, "Well, there's in-vitro fertilization," and I said, "I'll do that." I then went to my bedroom and wrote a manifesto in my journal swearing that I would never partake in sexual intercourse. The proclamation read:

I, Gloria Elizabeth Amodeo, will never ever ever ever ever ever ever ever ever ever ever have sex!

Signed: Gloria Elizabeth Amodeo

Six years later, when I turned thirteen, I went through that old journal and read that, and many other proclamations I had once made, such as *Don't tell anyone, but I still kind of like Barney* and *I'm a Pink Power Kid and my Power Ranger parents are going to save me.* I took a pen, drew an X through entries I no longer believed, and wrote the word *Retired*.

With that, the celibacy entry was discharged from duty.

By the time I entered college, I hadn't been revolted by the idea of sex for a long time. In high school, Ben, Morgan, and I watched softcore porn in the form of R or NC-17 rated movies. We went to our local VHS rental store and took out films like *Monster's Ball* and *Eyes Wide Shut*. Ben would steal the remote control and rewind when a sex scene finished, sometimes going back as many as six times to cement the naked, gyrating images in our brains.

"Ben! Ew!" Morgan and I would say. We pretended to be engrossed in the narrative, because girls weren't supposed to like sex scenes.

But I did like sex scenes, and I liked them more when they were real. Freshman year of high school, I was at a friend's house when she brought me into the family computer room and turned on a massive Dell desktop. "Do you want to see something funny?" she asked, and proceeded to pull up a porn website that her boyfriend had introduced her to, saying that she'd learn how to give a good blow job from it. "But these pictures are hilarious!" she said, scrolling through them.

I said, "Oh my God, so hilarious!" I thought, *I must visit this website instantly when I get home.*

That night, when my family was asleep, I snuck down to the computer room and masturbated to as many porn clips as I could.

Porn, I thought, turned me into a different person. When I wasn't thinking about porn, I was a nice, awkward girl who was happy to sit on the couch and watch Pippin the hobbit sing to Denethor about the end of all things. Sex seemed like the last thing on my mind.

Then the thought of porn would hit, and I was ravenous for boobs.

Despite all this, I was happy to keep my sex life a part of my secret imagination. I fantasized about unbuttoning the pants of guys I had crushes on and wrapping my legs around their waists, but something about that felt like it would change me, make me someone I didn't know how to be. When I watched porn, I felt stimulated at the sight of an unclothed woman, wondering what it would be like to feel and kiss her—but letting myself do that would turn me into a lesbian and make me even more of an outcast than I already was. I didn't want to turn into anything or anyone else. So I let sex exist in my imagination, in a place that was only for me.

The evangelical Christian notion of abstaining from sex until marriage was, at first, neither foreign nor uncomfortable to me. It was one of the tenets that initially attracted me to Cru, because I felt unprepared for a union between two bodies and figured that I would continue to feel that way until the day I got married. Evangelical Christianity taught that if I wasn't married, sex shouldn't exist in my mind at all. If it did, I would be betraying my future husband, because, according to Cru's reading of Matthew 5:28—"everyone who looks at a woman with lustful intent has already committed adultery with her in his heart"—imagining sex was the same as having it.

"You need to take every thought captive for Christ," Cate told me for the umpteenth time during one of our accountability sessions. I had just admitted my latest in a long line of sexual fantasies to her: that of peeling the clothes off my wildly good-looking next-door neighbor in the dorm. He was in a play with me and would often scoop me into hugs during rehearsals, kissing me on the forehead as his defined pectorals pressed against my chest. He'd recently told me that I had beautiful lips.

This dorm neighbor of mine was not only *not* my husband, he wasn't even Christian. It was a double-sin, in a sense, that I was fantasizing about him. I had long been told that I wasn't supposed to date men who weren't believers, lest I become "unequally yoked" with someone who did not know Christ. It's a term the apostle Paul uses in 2 Corinthians 6:14, referring to the distribution of weight between two oxen attached to the same yoke as they plow a field side by side. If one of those oxen isn't pulling its weight—i.e., living in Christ—the other can't move forward either. Dating someone like my neighbor, even though I wanted to, would have been like dating a dead person in Christianity's eyes. Not believing in Christ meant that he was "dead in [his] trespasses and sins" (Ephesians 2:1). It would be like tying myself to a corpse and dragging it around campus with me.

"You're going to need to talk about this on your Summer Project interview, you know," Cate said. "You'll have to give an account of your sexual history."

I remembered some of the questions I'd answered on my application, including one about whether or not I had experienced same-sex attraction.

"You mean they're going to ask me about that stuff?"

"Well, it won't be just anyone. It'll be another woman asking."

That didn't comfort me, since a large part of my sexual sin included being attracted to other women. I must have grown visibly flustered, because Cate asked if I had something to tell her. "No," I lied. "Just nervous."

"Why?" she asked.

"I don't know. It's just a lot." I then said something about how coming to know Jesus later in life meant developing habits that weren't necessarily righteous. My environment was not protected from certain sins—in fact, it was filled with them. My mother watched soap operas in front of me, with a ton of sex in them! How was I supposed to avoid being confused about it?

"Beth," Cate said. "It may help to tell me what's on your mind before your interview."

So, without praying or preparing or thinking it through, I told Cate, on the couch in the Cru room, that I liked porn, that I had been watching it for several years, and that I was attracted to the women I saw in it. The most terrifying part was her stillness as she listened to me, the way she seemed almost paralyzed as I told her something that I hadn't told anyone else.

"It makes me feel dirty," I concluded. "If the staff members knew, would they even want me around their children?"

"Please, please don't worry about anything like that," Cate

said. She told me that releasing this was a good thing, that I shouldn't be afraid to talk about it on my interview. She said that Summer Project would help me work through it, and she offered me a vision of the future: "I see you speaking at events and helping other women who struggle with homosexuality."

Struggle with homosexuality. According to Cate, I wasn't homosexual. I had a homosexual habit, like biting my nails. She said that more people needed to know about this part of me, because it would help me stay away from porn.

"Do I need to make an announcement or something?" I asked.

"No! But you should share this with Tara."

Great. Perky, girly Tara. Just the type of female I wanted to share my gayness with.

When I told Tara, she was empathetic, but unfazed.

"I struggle with the same thing," she admitted to me. "It's because my mom used to walk around naked when I was little."

"Really?" I was shocked. My mother did the same thing! She used to make me Eggos in the toaster oven with no clothes on, drinking instant coffee.

The more I talked about my same sex attraction to Cate and Tara, the more I heard that my experience wasn't an anomaly. I had masturbated since my earliest memories, which began when I was three, but Cate said little kids masturbated all the time. "I learned that in my teaching classes. They figure it out somehow." I had been attracted to both women and men just as long, but Tara said that was normal for little girls who grew up with messed-up mothers. "A part of her was distant, so you drew closer to females. It was the same thing for me. It's all a result of sin."

The main message I got from them was that there was hope. I could be healed from it if I simply withheld these thoughts and actions from myself. The logic was much less damning than I expected, and it was fed to me gently. I would be understood and accepted as long as I bought into it.

"Just be honest in your interview," Tara said. "God doesn't hate you for it."

✷

When I went to my first under-twenty-one nightclub, at the age of fifteen, I learned that men could touch me without my permission.

I had told my parents I was going to a birthday party, wearing a heavy jacket over my pink halter top as I ran out the door. My friend decked me out at her place before we left—hair up, thick eyeliner, fake lashes, glitter. My goal was simple: dance with a guy and kiss him. I had never had a boyfriend, but my curiosity was growing. I wanted to make out with someone, to see if I would like it. Would another person find me attractive enough to kiss back?

When we arrived, we saw a line of men against a wall. They swayed as the music boomed. We walked past them and I felt a squeeze on my butt—and then another and another. The whole line grabbed and painfully pinched my ass. I had come there to be physical, to dance with and kiss a stranger, but what I received was out of the range of what I thought men would do.

I tried to make sense of it by blaming my outfit. My back was exposed, so I looked too inviting. I was wearing tight pants and that's why they touched me. It was a new thought—that my clothes could be magnetic, and something could happen to my body that I had not welcomed with words.

I see now that part of me joined the church because I didn't want to have another experience like that again. I didn't want to worry about being touched without permission, about men coming up from behind me and rubbing against my body. I wanted a respectable womanhood, to be seen as a person, to be cared for by anyone who would want to be my lover. In the secular world, I worried that sex in the wrong context would take my humanity away. Evangelical Christianity promised a context in which, if I played by its rules, that wouldn't happen.

So I did what Cate and Cru told me. I made my clothes looser, hiked my pants higher, wore tank tops under long-sleeved shirts so they weren't see-through, so my cleavage didn't show. I did it to protect myself, to keep men from wanting me, to maintain my dignity and humanity in the only way I knew how.

It began to fall apart for the first time when I was studying abroad in England.

I found myself at a dance club again, this time at age nineteen, with a self-assurance that had grown because of God's affirmation during my morning runs. I went to the floor with Cate and Hannah, and we giggled in our female-only dance circle, mirroring each other's moves, framing our faces.

Then a guy appeared beside me. He had a shaved head and a cute face, tattoo sleeves up each arm. "Would you like to dance?" he asked.

I looked to Hannah, who was already dancing with another guy, and then to Cate, who gave me a look that said, *Are you sure you can handle this?*

I'm fine, I mouthed, and went off with the gentleman.

We danced for the rest of the night. He'd put his hands on my waist and tried to bring his pinkies to my hips, and I'd pull them back up, even though I liked the way they felt there. It felt good to be desired by someone I found attractive, to flirt with physical connection just shy of overt sexuality.

At the end of the night, when we were dancing to "Don't Stop Me Now," he leaned in to my ear and said, "Aren't you going to kiss me?"

Surprised by his forwardness, I answered, "No!"

"Why not?"

"Because . . . because I don't know you!"

"Oh! I'm Brad from Banbury!"

We continued to dance in circles and he took my hands, twirling me toward himself and away, holding his arm up so I could spiral.

"I still don't know you!" I said.

"You're crazy!" he laughed. "You only live once!"

At the time, I thought, *Well, yes, and I don't want to regret it.* But now I realize that I couldn't see what he was saying. In that moment, two wills battled inside of me—one that wanted to give and receive, and another that said it was dangerous. I had found myself a situation where I didn't feel objectified, where I felt connected and engaged, no matter how fleeting the interaction. But I didn't want to break the rules, and if I kissed him, that's what I would be doing. I would be giving something to Brad from Banbury that belonged to my future husband.

✷

The interview for Summer Project happened in the back of a building at my college. I sat on a stone wall, cell phone pressed to my ear. The interviewer was a well-respected staff member at Cru. She traveled all over the country lecturing about biblical womanhood and was, according to other staff members, exactly the type of woman I should aspire to be.

She began our call by praying that God would guide our conversation. Then she asked for my testimony, the steps that led to my conversion. I told her about my previous agnosticism and belief that the Bible was a load of crap until I met Cate, who convinced me that it wasn't. She asked me if I believed the Bible was infallible, God-breathed scripture. I told her absolutely. She asked if I knew how to get to heaven. I told her there was only one way, and that was through belief in Jesus Christ as Lord and Savior. She was gut-checking me. She wanted to make sure I was a *real* Christian.

About halfway through the conversation, my sexual history came up. "I see here on your application that you've experienced same-sex attraction."

"Yes. But not exclusively. I'm attracted to men, too."

"Have you kissed or experienced heavy petting with another woman?"

"No. Just in my head."

"In your head?"

"I mean, I've imagined it."

"You've also engaged in masturbation and the viewing of pornography," she said.

"Yeah."

"How long?"

"Since I was thirteen."

"And when was the last time you did it?"

"About two weeks ago."

It was like being questioned by a doctor. *When was your last period? How long have you had symptoms? Do you have a history of rashes?* I imagined the woman writing my responses down on a notepad and then stewing over them at night, pacing around a mahogany desk as she tried to figure out the cure for my ailment.

"You'll be sharing a room with two other women," she said in summation. "You won't be allowed to do any of that in front of them."

Like hunger, I have found sex to be primal, but even when I am eating, I am still me. I can eat food with a friend at a picnic and share jokes about the day, the news, the past. Eating does not make me lose the sense of self I have built over time. It does not open me up so all the atoms spill out, disorganized, with no direction, much less propriety. Rather, it operates as an extension of my humanity. I eat because I am human. I eat because it's natural.

Sex is the same, but when I sat on that stone wall, I didn't know that yet. I didn't know, as I was warned against masturbating in front of my future friends, that sex would not turn me into an animal. That one day I would experience sex uncontrolled, uncontained by the marriage her God created to restrain it, and I wouldn't lose myself inside of it. All I knew was that I needed to survive, and the church convinced me that I couldn't do that without following their instructions. I believed I needed more instruction to make it work, to help me get better at withholding things I wanted from myself.

✷

When I was taught about the verse in Matthew 5:28 that equated lust in the mind with sexual intercourse in reality, it was in the context of protecting our brothers in Christ. According to Cru, men were "visual creatures" by nature and objectified women innately, because God had created them that way. This was taught in exclusively female settings, such as Bible studies or discipling meetings or "women's time," in which women were separated from men and spoken to about "woman things" by other women. "Men want you!" a staff woman told us at an East Coast Cru conference, speaking on a microphone attached to her ear. "You have to be aware of that and protect them for their future wives."

After I'd been accepted into the Hampton Beach Summer Project but before it began, I was sitting on my parents' couch back in Southbridge, reading an email from the woman who had interviewed me. The message had been sent to all the women attending the project, with the subject line "Hampton Beach Dress Code—Please Read." Something about it seemed stern, much different from the fun "Get ready for the time of your life!" emails that we'd been receiving from the male staff members. What was inside, I thought, must be heavy.

I opened it and read a detailed instruction guide about what I was allowed to wear, and when, for my ten-week trip. Not only did my tank tops have to be thick enough to cover my bra straps, but I wasn't allowed to wear two-piece bathing suits if I chose to swim in the ocean. One-pieces were suggested, preferably with a T-shirt over them; if I *had* to wear a tank top, I should consider putting a T-shirt over it. Cleavage was forbidden, no matter how hot it got, and shorts had to be long, of the Bermuda variety. Also, no pajamas while downstairs with the men. Once we changed into our pajamas, we had to stay in the women's quarters.

All of this, it was explained, was to keep the hearts of our brothers in Christ safe from sexual sin. We needed to create an equal-opportunity space for spiritual growth, and that couldn't happen for the men if we were trying to avoid overheating.

I wondered if the men had gotten a similar email. *Keep your shirts on, gentleman. No flaunting your pecs for the ladies. We don't care how hot you get while playing soccer on the beach.* But mostly, I imagined what would happen if I didn't follow the rules, if I walked outside in that pink halter top again with fake lashes and glitter. I thought about how I wasn't that person anymore, how that person was inappropriate and unsafe. She was asking for what she got. She was lucky that much worse didn't happen to her—if she had compromised the spiritual walks of her future brothers in Christ, maybe she would have deserved it.

✷

Withholding in the evangelical community is about protection. You withhold to protect the hearts and bodies of yourself and others. Withholding results in rewards, because withholding is sacrifice. If you sacrifice your momentary desires for God, he will give you a good marriage. He will give you better sex than you would have had otherwise. Withholding is costly, but worth it in the end. It is worth it to give up what you wanted, what you thought would make you happy, and let God give you his best instead.

Or so I was told, over and over. What I wanted was not the best for me.

So I withheld.

There is guilt stitched to this form of withholding, into the very framework of what makes it effective. Having sex would disappoint God. I needed to abstain so he would be glad in me. *Hold back. Hold back. Hold back. It's good for you. You can't make your own decisions. You don't know what's best for you.*

Brad from Banbury said, "You only live once." I saw him one more time after the night we danced. Two days before I left England, my classmates and I were at a pub, and he spotted me from the other side of the bar. He smiled, raised his hand, and waved. I turned away and pretended I didn't recognize him. I was too frightened to admit I did, to let myself wave back.

With this type of withholding, there is a type of safety, but there is also unfathomable regret.

11.

When I arrived at the Hampton Beach Summer Project house, which we called the White Gull, I was given a blue T-shirt with an image of the state of New Hampshire on it and the state motto in cursive lettering: *Live Free or Die*. It was fitting, I thought, since we were trying to free people from spiritual death with the gospel. That's what the story was, or at least, that was the part of it that I needed to learn how to communicate effectively over the next ten weeks. The number one objective of Summer Project was to grow spiritually, and I would only be able to do that if I got used to obsessively sharing my faith.

I was also introduced to my summer discipler. Her name was Dana, and she was a staff member attending Project with her husband and children. Tan and friendly, Dana was fifteen years older than me but didn't look it. "Let me show you to your room," she said, and brought me up two flights of stairs, to a nook with bunk beds, a spare bed, and an attached bathroom. "Your roommates haven't arrived yet, but we've prayed for you all. I think you'll like them. You're all older girls."

Older girls? I was twenty-one. Was I getting old?

My roommates arrived while I was unpacking. The first to get there was Cam, her hair covered in a bandana. She wore basketball shorts and an oversized T-shirt and had a well-defined jaw that made her look tough when she chewed gum. "Hey," she said, swinging her hand out to shake. "Cam." She lifted a foot and balanced casually on one leg, her presence masculine with a side of jitters. I shook her hand and said, "Beth," and then she asked if she could take the top bunk.

"Can't wait to meet our other roommate," Cam said. "Did you know she's married?"

Jennifer arrived next, flustered, with a rolling suitcase in tow. She was Afro-Latina, the fifth and final person of color I met on the whole project. (The other four had been recruited via our New Jersey sector of Cru.) She had long, lustrous hair that she clipped up halfway. I stared at her diamond wedding ring, and as the days went on, she let me ask her questions about sex.

"Does it hurt the first time?"

"Yeah. It still kind of does."

"But is it enjoyable?"

"Heck yes! You get to see his sexy body!"

As Dana predicted, Cam, Jennifer, and I bonded quickly. We taped a list of room rules to the wall that included "No audible farting" and farted audibly anyway, as loud as we possibly could. We made breakfast together on the weekends and dinner at night, splitting groceries and making monstrous twelve-egg omelets. We talked until we fell asleep and shared the stories of our lives, going late into the night even though we had to get up early.

And by "early," I mean four o'clock a.m. One of the requirements of the Hampton Beach Summer Project was that we had to get summer jobs so that we could evangelize to our coworkers. This was meant to prepare us for the professional world, when our jobs would be our mission fields. Most project attendees got jobs at McDonald's or Dunkin Donuts, while a few worked at an arcade on the boardwalk. Cru was giving us a chance to work out our witnessing kinks on the staff of fast-food chains, figuring out how to tell the gospel story best while multitasking over a hot grill. No matter the job, the goal was the same: learn how to build God's kingdom in any setting.

On the first day of Project, we congregated downstairs, where we were instructed on how to carry out this master plan.

"You'll need to memorize the *Knowing God Personally* booklet," Dana's husband said, "because you most likely won't be able to fit it in your work pants."

I glanced at the screen door as a white airport van pulled in. The van door slid open and a young man got out, dark curly hair covering his head. He carried a guitar out of the van, and was wearing a white sweatshirt and white-washed jeans. A little geeky, but still kind of cute. Then he turned around and I saw his face. Dark brows over big, brooding eyes, with cheekbones resting below. Full, almost puckered lips. I couldn't imagine not falling in love with him.

✷

Before Project, I'd had a crush on an evangelical Christian guy. His name was Mark, and I'd fallen for him two years earlier, when he showed up at the church Cate and I attended. I told her about him immediately, as she'd been starting to get annoyed when I complained that I didn't find Christian men emotionally attractive. "I have a crush on one!" I announced to her. Cate was, at last, happy with me. "See?" she said. "Christian guys aren't all weird!"

The crush, at first, was less based on his personality and more on his appearance—he looked like James McAvoy, who played Mr. Tumnus in *The Chronicles of Narnia*. Same distinguished nose, same small mouth that grew into a large, clean smile. He was a bit awkward socially, like a nervous homeschooled kid, laughing a little too loud at jokes and cracking his own that weren't funny. He was a *good* boy, but not a *cool* boy. I thought a few months in the real world, away from his small hometown, would probably even him out. I turned out to be right, as Mark made friends and became more fluid in his social interactions, laughing at the appropriate volume at appropriate times, and even making his own jokes.

When I got re-baptized, Mark was there. I say "re-baptized" because I had already been baptized as a baby, in the Catholic church my parents raised me in. My soul had been promised to that version of God with my head over a bowl, a seashell scooping water onto my baldness. Cate made it clear that this first baptism didn't count. Baptism was something you chose—not something your parents selected for you when you were two months old.

On the Sunday that my rebaptism happened, I was instructed to wear a bathing suit underneath an expendable pair of shorts and a dark, solid-colored T-shirt. I proclaimed my testimony as Mark, in the front row, beamed. Was I getting baptized for God, or was I doing it for Mark? When I stepped into the pool, the pastor told me to get on my knees and hold my nose. He put a hand on the back of my head, another on the wrist in front of my face. He counted to three, and then dunked me. I emerged from the water soaked, gasping for air like a newborn baby, with two hundred people cheering.

✷

One morning, Mark messaged me on Facebook, asking if Cate and I were going to be at an event that evening.

Holy mother of pearl! Did he like me back?

Messages about Cate's and my presence at various events continued, and I started to get my hopes up. Maybe God was sending me a husband! Mark seemed to want to hang out all the time, texting me about getting ice cream and seeing movies and playing board games.

Then Cate broke the news to me. "Mark messaged me," she said. "He wants to grab coffee this week."

I still held a sliver of hope that I was the reason for this, that he was using Cate as a buffer to learn more about me, asking her to get together so he could discover the key to my heart. But I knew better. No decent single man in the evangelical world would ask a woman to hang out one-on-one if he wasn't interested in her.

"Are you going to do it?" I asked.

"I think so. Are you comfortable with that?"

"I don't know."

"I just want to see what he says. I won't decide to date him without talking to you."

While Mark and Cate went on their coffee date, I busied myself in classwork, buried my head in a play, trying to think about anything other than the two of them together. *I'm beautiful*, I tried to tell myself. *God thinks so. Even if Mark doesn't see it, that doesn't mean I'm not.* It was a story that didn't ring true in all the corners of my soul.

✷

On the first day of project, Dana took Cam, Jennifer, and me to the beach and told us to share our testimonies with one another. She asked us only to share what we were comfortable sharing, "but also," she added, "be brave."

She went first, to set an example. She told us how she had grown up in a Christian home and accepted Jesus when she was a young child, like most of the kids around her. She began to question her faith as a teenager, but ultimately continued her relationship with the Lord as she got "plugged in" to good ministries in college. She met her husband through Campus Crusade, who was a bit hot-and-cold when they were dating, breaking up with her before asking her to marry him. Now they were happily married with children.

Cam went next. She told us how she had been adopted as a baby. While her adoptive parents took her to church, the knowledge that she had been given up by her birth parents took a toll. As a result, she started smoking weed in high school, as well as having sex and experimenting with harder drugs. She became "a shell of a person," neither living or dead. She eventually came back to Jesus after seeing a demon in a dream, which scared her so much that she stopped doing drugs and broke off her sexual relationships. She became involved with Campus Crusade and had been sober ever since.

Finally, some real stuff, I thought.

Jennifer went next. She told us about the Pentecostal church she had grown up in, in which she'd been forced to wear skirts and head coverings. Sexual abuse was rampant in the congregation, and she had had many terrible experiences before finally breaking free. She studied the Bible on her own and decided that wearing pants would be fine in the eyes of God and that the theological argument for women wearing head coverings in church was weak on a contextual level. When she entered college, she got involved in Campus Crusade and began experiencing churches other than the one she'd grown up in. She was glad to be at Project and have the chance to grow spiritually, despite the lead staff members being concerned that ten weeks was too long for her to be away from her husband. "He's visiting every two weeks," she said. "We worked out a deal so our marriage stays healthy."

After hearing Cam and Jennifer, I felt comfortable enough to share my story—warts and all, including the pornography parts I had given up cold turkey. I told them about my mother and the ways in which she was sick, as well as about my little sister and the urgency of their salvation. I shared my newness in the faith and how I still felt like a baby Christian, how hard it was to learn all this as an adult and feel at least five spiritual steps behind other believers my age.

"You don't seem that way at all," Cam said. "I'd never think that."

"Yeah," Jennifer said. "You have so much wisdom even speaking right now."

The storytelling didn't end that day. It went on for the whole ten weeks as we insisted on knowing everything we could about each other. The broken parts of ourselves melded together and formed the bond we needed to grow. We saw our own stories in each other—a God-centered kinship.

✷

I didn't have many interactions with August, the curly-haired guy I'd seen getting out of the van, until we practiced for the Summer Project worship team together. Four of us had been selected based on our musical talents: Cam on drums, August on bass, me on vocals, and a skinny-jeaned kid named Louis on acoustic guitar. Our main responsibility was to put a set list together to lead everyone in worship at our weekly meetings; we'd sing a couple of songs, listen to announcements, sit through a teaching, and then sing a few more songs and worship, worship, worship.

During rehearsals, I learned that August was from the South and was cerebral to the core, moved entirely by logic, reminiscent of Cate in the way he interacted with the people around him. Like me, he hadn't been born into a family of believers. "I came to know Christ in college," he said, when we sat in a circle and shared our testimonies. Here was someone who could understand me like no one else.

At first, August didn't seem to show any of the interest in me that I felt for him. There was not so much as a look or an acknowledgment of my presence other than moving aside if I was walking past him. I kept my attraction quiet at the beginning, not even writing about it in my journal, for fear my heart would go haywire and I'd lose my concentration on God. "Guard your hearts, ladies," a phrase torn from Proverbs 4:23, was one of the main messages that Naomi taught in our women's-time sessions.

I tried to stick my brain in the Bible. I told myself to ignore August during mixed-gender meetings and focus my attention on Cam and Jennifer instead. The goal, I surmised, was to become as aloof as possible, because the more aloof I was, the less hurt I'd get in the end. I wanted so badly to be a woman who could control her thoughts, who didn't fantasize the life out of her romantic future, who wasn't hyper-aware of all the possibilities in her surroundings.

And then, August started to notice me.

The first time was over a pile of pancake mix. Cam, Jennifer, and I were in the kitchen downstairs, trying to figure out how to keep the mix from sticking to the pan. August appeared and offered to help. We strategized. Should we use Pam or butter, and how high should the heat be? Should we scorch it or simmer? How long would each side take? Though we lost half the batch to premature flipping, we enjoyed enough pancakes to fill us up, and after that, August took a shine to me.

For two weeks straight, he made a beeline to me in meetings. He sat next to me and chatted me up and chuckled over what I said. I realized that although he was serious, he was also very funny, with a sense of humor complementary to mine. He wasn't afraid to make weird noises or faces, to let himself look ridiculous. He knew how to be the butt of a joke and make people laugh with him. He was intelligent, well-read, quoting philosophers in regular conversation. He struggled through his faith openly, admitting his doubts about God but vowing to believe in him nevertheless. I was captivated.

One night, I sat on a porch swing in front of the house we were staying in, taking in the salty air with a Bible on my lap. It had been a long, tedious day at McDonald's, and I needed a moment with God, a moment to center myself and get August out of my head. Of course, he showed up.

"It's chilly out here," he said. "Aren't you cold?"

"A little," I said. "Just suffering for God, I guess."

He laughed and asked what I was reading, and I told him Ecclesiastes, my favorite book of the Bible. He asked what I liked about it, and I told him it spoke what I thought. "What has been is what will be, and what has been done is what will be done, and there is nothing new under the sun" (Ecclesiastes 1:9).

"Dark," August said.

"Sure. But it's truth."

We stayed out together for half an hour. I wanted to run on the beach with him, take a walk down the shore and come back after the sun emerged. I wanted to hold his hand, see what it felt like, if it was dry or damp, if there were pillows on his palm or fingers.

The next night, the staff announced that they would be leaving the project. It had been five weeks, and we were now tasked with taking the mission over ourselves. August was named the new project leader.

✷

My summer project job at McDonald's siphoned the energy out of me. I was a register girl who was not very good on the registers; the menu system allowed eight different ways of entering an order, but management wanted us to do it only one way. I could never remember how to do it, which led them to put me in the drive-thru window, where I stood alone, swiping credit cards. Bored out of my mind, I couldn't stop fantasizing about August.

I used to think that a story could be true even if I imagined it. Who was the arbiter of what happened and what didn't? I could experience something just as real in my mind. "You've never kissed a boy," Desiree Wharton said to me in junior high. "Uh, yes I have," I answered. I had kissed Prince Harry a million times as I fell asleep. I was very experienced.

When Christianity came along, I understood that I would have been lying if I said I wasn't a virgin, if I claimed Prince Harry as my lover from the ages of eleven to seventeen. But at the same time, in this new Christian version of reality, the birth of Jesus was true, and so was his resurrection. He would come again to judge the living and the dead. Belief in this story was the difference between spiritual life and death.

I didn't know what story to believe about August. One day, after work, I went out onto the beach with a blanket and a Bible in hand, praying, *God, please bring me closer to you.* I read pieces of the gospels, the stories of Jesus walking through the world as a man. I asked God how I was supposed to let these stories fill me when the stories I made up in my head were far more compelling and relevant to my life. I felt like a bad Christian, like a failure in his eyes, because I could not stop trying to write my own life's story.

Give it to me, I heard him say. *Let me write it. Believe it or not, I'm a better writer than you.*

I wanted to believe it, but I also wanted to have a say. I wanted to have something dangerous, something that Cru had been warning against: the ability to control my own life.

✷

August and I went to church that summer with a woman named Barbara, who was filled with the most amazing, almost unbelievable stories. She claimed that Dan Brown had spent a year at her church getting inspiration for *The Da Vinci Code,* and that she saw spirits. "I saw my husband when he was a boy," she said. "Back before I knew the Lord, his spirit sat on my bed." She had many tales to tell, of struggle and strife, of a life before Jesus filled with drugs and abuse. Throughout it all, she said, she'd always had the gift of prophecy. She had visions of the future and of other people's pasts.

"You two are special," she said one evening, pointing at August and me, and I wondered if a vision had just passed before her eyes.

A week later, our Summer Project put on a dance with a "five-dollar prom" theme. I got a horrible pink dress at a thrift store and wore it with a large red belt. Cam and I put plastic water bottles on our heads and secured our hair over them with hairspray and elastics to simulate updos. We formed kick lines and did the conga all over a rented high school hall.

At one point August approached me, wearing blue shorts up to his nipples.

"Can we talk?"

We walked outside together. It was happening, it was really happening. Was he going to express his feelings for me? Was my life story going to transform into my fantasies?

He brought me to a park across the street with monuments of cannons, something that commemorated a war.

"I think it's time I told you that I've been interested in you," August said. "You're so thoughtful. I appreciate each word you say." He told me he found me incredibly attractive, not just for my looks but because I was a "leader among women."

And those words built a story in my mind so strong that I didn't know how to hear anything else that he said. I saw marriage as he explained that he didn't want a long-distance relationship, that he didn't believe something like that could work.

The next morning at church, Barbara told me to follow her outside. "August talked to you last night, didn't he? I sensed it when you came in this morning. God made you for each other, but just know that he's a man set apart by the Lord. You'll have to give up your dreams if you want to have a life with him."

After her coffee date with Mark, Cate had asked me to the cafeteria. "He told me that he likes me," she'd said, confirming both of our suspicions. She promised that she wouldn't date him if I didn't want her to. Our friendship was the most important thing. I needed to search God's will in my heart. Whether or not she'd date him was, essentially, my decision. I took a week to think about it, to go through the pain of this indirect rejection. I was angry at her for putting it on me, for not just saying, "No, Mark. Dating you is out of the question." But I couldn't imagine God wanting me to keep Cate and Mark from being together. I could only imagine God wanting me to do away with my emotions, conquer them, silence them. To make less noise so he could make more. In the end, I told Cate I was okay with her dating Mark. It was not a true story, but it was the story I thought I needed to tell.

When August told me that I was a leader among women, that he hung on my words and appreciated my mind, it felt like a new story was emerging, one where I received the best possible outcome. In this situation, I didn't have to wait for my love interest to grow up and become perfect for me—he already was, from the very moment he had stepped out of that van. He felt tailored for me, my great reward for holding on to my virginity for so long.

Life was changing. August had admitted his attraction to me, and Barbara had prophesied that we were meant to be together. I had two new best friends in Cam and Jennifer. When the summer ended, I was going to live a big, grand life as a grad student in New York City. Was this, at last, what waiting for God's best looked like?

There are few hurdles too high to jump when we really love a story, when we want to see it come to life in the world around us. I remember telling the story of the gospel with August on the beach. I remember teaming up with him and sharing our faith with strangers. He'd tell the story and philosophically argue it when people questioned its logic, and I'd think, *I'm so glad we believe this. I'm so glad we have this story in common.* In my mind, it was the story that tied us together, the North Star of the days ahead that would heal our greatest sorrows. I never dreamed that it would one day be the greatest difference between us.

12.

Since I work in the advertising industry, I'm familiar with the definition of the word "vertical." As opposed to "horizontal marketing," which is supposed to have a broader appeal, "vertical marketing" is meant to appeal to a specific niche or demographic—middle-aged men, say, or people who work in real estate. Each of these niches is called a "vertical."

I can see now that evangelism was my first vertical marketing experience.

For example, when Cate encouraged me to become friends with the popular theater kids in college, I began to evangelize the hell out of my theater vertical. I responded in the affirmative to their text messages. I showed up at their dorms when they invited me over on the weekends, watching *P.S. I Love You* with them over microwaved nachos. At parties, when they were drunk and wanted to go to White Castle, I, always sober, drove them. When they threw up from drinking too much beer, I helped them eat white bread to soak up the alcohol. I slept on the ground with them and dreamed, talked about our futures and answered their questions about my faith. I was among them but not of them, as Jesus had instructed in John 17. I did not allow myself to give into the same earthly desires, but I met them where they were, with actions and messages tailored to them. I was the only one, Cate said, who they were allowing to reach them. They were my audience, and I had to do right by God and by them.

On Summer Project, we learned how to manage what I have come to realize were multiple verticals. These were the markets and submarkets that were personal to us—our family, friends, and coworkers. We were the chosen sales representatives, and if we didn't show these people Christ, who would? But it was not a strategy born in an advertising boardroom. It was grown in our hearts. Souls depended on it.

One day, we watched a YouTube clip of the magician Penn Jillette. He was an outspoken atheist, but he shared a story about a man who had given him a Bible after a show and how it made him think about evangelism. "How much do you have to hate somebody to not proselytize?" he said. "How much do you have to hate somebody to believe that everlasting life is possible and not tell them that? If I believed beyond a shadow of a doubt that a truck was coming at you and you didn't believe it, and that truck was bearing down on you, there's a certain point where I tackle you. And this is more important than that."

By the end of the video, we were all in tears, thinking about our personal verticals and how much we wanted to save them. I thought about my college theater friends, all the nonbelievers who had funded my trip, who loved me enough to give me the most they could. Did I have the guts to repay them, to give them the gift of the gospel that could lead to their eternal lives? Was I brave enough to share the truth with my coworkers at McDonald's?

Developing evangelism skills, I discovered, was less about learning strategies and more about cultivating a sense that I was in a burning building and that the fire would eat up everyone around me if I didn't try my hardest to get them out in time.

*

I of course thought most about my parents, who were still stuck in their stubborn unbelief. Did I have the strength to keep going, to not give up on them no matter how impossible their conversions seemed?

My father claimed to go vertical every night of the week. "I pray," he told me on the many car rides from New Jersey in which I'd try to convert him. "Every night. All the time. I love Jesus! I really do."

He'd grown up in Albany, New York, with a Sicilian father and a German mother, attending Catholic school with nuns as teachers until he entered college. He knew all the rules of the Bible, he told me, but after having them emotionally beaten into him in a way that seemed to contradict what he had read of God's love, he found it less confusing to treat Christianity as a religious buffet that he could pick and choose from. I hated Catholicism for this reason, for the way it screwed with my father's ability to truly hear and understand the gospel I was sharing.

His main problem, I believed, was his proclivity to do things himself. He was too terrified to let God, or anyone else for that matter, step in and take over. He had built the majority of our house by himself—all the cabinets, the whole roof—and was handy when it came to fixing cars. As a teenager, he was an amateur pilot and a skilled sailor who sailed around Lake Champlain. Septic system broken? He would take care of it. Leak in the ceiling? Don't you even dare think of calling anyone else! He loved his handyman identity and spent many mornings during my childhood tinkering away in his basement woodshop before we'd wake up and beg him to make us Belgian waffles—which he did well. Why pay someone to do it, he always said, when you can do it yourself?

My father has always been a good boy—a kind, genial person with a certain innocence that seems to follow him wherever he goes. He's only been drunk a handful of times and never tried drugs, telling people in college who'd try to pressure him (to his future children's deep embarrassment), "Listen, if I want to get high, I just get in my plane." He's spent many an evening at the homes of coworkers, teaching them to change their oil or unclog their toilets. If your car breaks down on the side of the road, my father will stop to help you. He's that kind of a person.

It all made it so hard to convert him.

"I'm a good person!" he'd say. "I've never done a bad thing. I don't deserve hell!"

"Daddy, we all deserve hell. Humanity does because of what happened at the Fall."

"What are you talking about? I never fell."

I tried to market Christianity to my father by emphasizing Jesus, who he seemed to think was a great guy.

"Jesus is wonderful," he'd say.

"Yes, he is," I'd answer, hopeful.

"And I bet you he was a man just like me. I wouldn't be surprised if he took a wife at some point." Damn *The Da Vinci Code* and the ideas it put in my father's head.

My father's perfectionistic nature caused many issues between him and my mother, issues that I tried and failed to fix. He accused my mother of being lazy, of not helping out around the house. "Here I am filling up the dishwasher again," he'd grumble. "Oh, and look, I have to fold the laundry, too."

"Mom, why don't you help out?" I would say to her, folding underwear and trying to mediate.

"Because your father will just do it all over again." She pointed to my folding job. "You're wasting your time with that. He wants it done a certain way."

If my father converted, I thought, it would trickle down to my whole family. His actions toward my mother would change, and he'd get over his my-way-or-the-highway approach. She'd feel loved, not useless, welcomed into the fold of her marriage, and she'd begin to attend church with him, curious to see what had changed her husband. In turn, God would change her, getting her off the pills, and then my sisters and brother would be in awe and quickly give their lives to the Lord, too.

My father was the key, the vertical to change all verticals, and I dreamed of the day when God would step into his life, when he would choose to do away with Dan Brown's Jesus and follow the real one.

*

I was not the only Summer Project member who worked at my McDonald's location. Joining me was Maggie, the moodiest girl on our mission. I quickly learned not to speak to her on our six a.m. drives over to the restaurant. One time, when I said good morning to her, she walked out the door without me, letting it slam in my face. But then her mood might shift without warning, going from downtrodden to chipper in a matter of seconds.

Maggie had had a troubled life before her relationship with Christ began, and while she now believed in Jesus, she wasn't exactly what Cate would have called "solid." She was dating a non-Project member who she'd make out with. She even told me that she'd take her shirt off in his car when things got particularly steamy. That was against Project rules, but I didn't rat her out. I told myself it was between her and God.

We had a nice manager at McDonald's ("I always like you Summer Project kids! So obedient!") and an assistant manager who insinuated that we were stupid for not realizing on our first day that we had to clock in at register one before going further behind the counter. On the grill with Maggie was a trans man named Reese—though at the time, neither Maggie nor I knew the word *trans*. While we had both come from colleges with gay and lesbian students, neither of us had ever met anyone who had openly changed their outward gender. We knew that Reese "identified" as a man and dated women exclusively, and we knew enough from church teachings that this wouldn't be favorable in God's eyes, because God was all about his natural order and creation and so he probably meant it when he assigned someone a gender. But how could we say this to Reese?

Reese became our favorite person at McDonald's, only taking his job seriously enough to get it done. He made the repetition of the job enjoyable, dancing as he flipped burgers and wiped mushrooms off the grill. At the end of his shift, he'd unbutton his work shirt and let it flow like some sort of cape as he walked out the door.

He wanted to hang out with us on our days off, and Maggie and I wanted to bring him to church so we could figure out how to love this new vertical in the way that God wanted us to. How much would we have to hate him not to try?

✷

Our Summer Project house, the White Gull, had only four parking spots. This meant we had a limited number of cars to do necessary life things with, which in turn meant that one day I got trapped in a car fighting about Calvinism with Adam Reynolds.

Calvinism, I had learned, taught the doctrine of predestination, which was what Patricia, the anti-abortion woman at the church I had taken my sister to, had tried to push on me in the early days of my faith. It said that God predestined people for either heaven or hell before they were born, that he didn't let them make their own decisions because there was no way he could. As the creator of all things, how could he let the thoughts of his creations out of his control and still call himself God?

When I said that I kind of liked Arminianism—an alternate theological teaching that saw God as a giver of free will, allowing humans to choose or reject him—Adam told me it wasn't biblically sound because Romans 9 said that God had "prepared [believers] beforehand for glory."

Oh, he wants to spar, I thought, and pointed out 1 Timothy 2:4, in which Paul wrote that God "desires all people to be saved and to come to the knowledge of the truth."

Adam said that I was interpreting the text too simply, that what God *wanted* and what God *decreed* were often separate. He brought up the concept of grace, which evangelicalism taught was God's act of giving us things we didn't deserve (like salvation, and his love) and said that if we *chose* to accept Jesus into our hearts, that meant we had done something to deserve his salvation, which was a biblical impossibility.

My mind went to my father. Had God predestined him to be saved? What if he hadn't? Was that why my father couldn't get over his *Da Vinci Code* version of Jesus?

I told Adam that wasn't a God that anyone should believe in, and that's when the car erupted as the other passengers revealed that they agreed with Adam. It became clear to me that I was not allowed to believe in the concept of free will in good conscience.

When we got back to the house, I found August on the couch in the living room, Bible open as he studied, hand stroking the plentiful hair on his chin.

"Why do you look so upset?" he said, and I told him about Calvinism and how I thought it was the most abominable teaching I had ever learned.

"It's biblical, though," he said. "There's way more precedence for it than Arminianism."

Really? I thought. *August too?*

Adam stopped by my room later that day and offered to let me borrow his copy of Wayne Grudem's *Systematic Theology*. "This will help you understand," he said.

But I didn't want to understand. I wanted to reject. This way of thinking wasn't what I signed up for—it didn't shake hands with the loving God in my head who had been growing larger and more beautiful during my mission, filling me with hope as I prayed for the people I loved. How much would I have to hate somebody to share this version of God with them?

I went out to the beach with my Bible and prayed, read Romans 9 ten times and journaled about my anger at the apostle Paul:

Paul bothers me a lot sometimes. His arguments can be really weak and unhelpful. I'm never going to become a Calvinist, but it turns out that August is one. If there's any chance of him and I being together and that makes him turn away from me, well—he can just find some other girl, I guess.

Like a rebuke from Paul's grave, I read Romans 9:20–21: "But who are you, O man, to answer back to God? Will what is molded say to its molder, 'Why have you made me like this?' Has the potter no right over the clay, to make out of the same lump one vessel for honorable use and another for dishonorable use?" Dishonorable use, the commentary said, was the equivalent of being made into a trash can.

It really bothers me that someone else had to be a garbage receptacle for your glory to shine brighter on me, I wrote. *Why evangelize? Why love or care about anyone who is not a believer? Why even bother if we are all robots anyways? PLEASE! You, who have followed me around and loved me forEVER, help me understand you!!!*

I cried as I wrote and spilled tears onto the page and watched the ink fuzz. Was this what graduating from spiritual milk to spiritual meat felt like? Like growing knives for teeth? Like bleeding internally? No spiritual teaching had disturbed me so profoundly, had bumped up so violently against my spirit, had made me come back swinging quite so hard.

I pushed my Bible and journal away. *No more words,* I felt God say, and I rolled onto my back. I looked up at the fading sky through sunglasses and imagined myself giving in, imagined what it would be like to let myself agree. To say, "This is the way God works and it goes against human understanding." To be content with not understanding, to change my prayers accordingly. To go from "God, help me lead this person to you" to "God, show me your will for this person in this moment."

I closed my eyes and heard *I love you, I love you. I am for you, not against you. I will be with you in every room.* No words of self-defense, no insecurity in God's voice as he held me through my pain, through the turmoil in my heart. The wind from the ocean traveled over me in a blanket of sensation, and in the silence was rest, a peace that surpassed all understanding.

Was it similar to the moment when I accepted Christ three years before? Was it the culmination of striving to understand and not being able to? Did I see myself gaining more from giving in and agreeing with the people around me than trying to fight for what I felt was true? At the time, it felt like I was being scooped up by the wind, into the arms of something much greater than myself. There was not a time in those early days of my faith when taking my problems to God did not validate what others had already been telling me. God never negated whatever doctrine I was resisting, didn't ask me to speak out against the people who had encouraged me to pray. Rather, he showed me that I was the stubborn one. I was the one who couldn't see. I needed to submit myself to learning.

I shut my anger off and went back into the beach house, into the company of people who would accept me that much more if I loved the exact same God they did.

*

As Cate spent a very different summer dating my former crush Mark, a slew of new Cates took over my heart. August, Adam,

Cam, Jennifer, even Maggie in her grumpiness—they formed a community around me and became the ones who knew me, the ones who kept me accountable in my moments of greatest struggle—intellectual, emotional, and even physical at times, as I admitted to Cam and Jennifer that I couldn't stop imagining sex with August. They acted as my accountability partners, helping me to take my thoughts captive. My friendship verticals were expanding further, away from Cate and into new territory. New minds, new perspectives, new experiences—new ways of showing love, sometimes more compatible with mine than Cate's had been.

Cam would catch me in the morning before I left for work, while she was getting ready for her job at Dunkin' Donuts, tucking her shirt in. "I love you, man," she'd whisper. Jennifer found out about my dislike for low-hanging pants—not because of modesty per se, but because I hated seeing people's butt cracks. When I did anything in the kitchen, from washing dishes to making a sandwich, she'd organize a line of women with their backs to me. I'd turn around and be greeted with a row of butt cracks. I would then run away as they chased me around the top floor of the house, laughing so hard it felt like my lungs would burst.

When I entered "the Tampico Challenge"—a contest we created which involved drinking an entire gallon of Tampico fruit punch—Jennifer kneeled beside me the whole time, like a ringside boxing coach. "You can do this," she said. "Go slow." When my stomach had had enough, she yelled, "Make way! Let Beth inside!" as I ran in through the sliding door and threw up all over the kitchen. Cam was already on the ground with a roll of paper towels, cleaning up my mess. "You're okay! Get back out there!" Jennifer said, bringing me outside so I could finish the jug and achieve Tampico glory.

I wanted the whole world to have what I had in those moments, friends who I could puke in front of without embarrassment, who told me they loved me each morning and helped me get back in the world when I was down. I saw it as a blessing to be part of God's family, to share this rawness as well as this enlightenment. We'd never be alone as we sought the heart of God together. My isolation was over, and I was having so much fun.

✷

A few weeks before Summer Project ended, Maggie and I asked August for his godly advice about Reese, our trans coworker.

"So she's gay," he said.

"Not she, he," Maggie said.

"Okay, she wants to be a he," August said. "Man, that's tough. I don't even know what to do about that!"

We hadn't expected to stump August. We thought that the staff leaders would have at least left him with some sort of protocol on this type of thing.

"Let me meet him," August said. "Have him over to the house."

We invited Reese to the White Gull. When he got there, Maggie and I sat with him on the porch swing. He complimented our porch and seemed comfortable despite our nervousness, the voices of the staff members in our heads telling us that he was living in sin and we needed to address that in some way. That *way*, we thought, was by bringing him to the feet of August, the wisest and smartest man on Project who had a special relationship with God. Let God talk through August, let him astound us with his insight. Let him, at the very least, plant a cosmic seed in Reese.

When August walked out to meet us, he shook Reese's hand, and Maggie and I took our leave, claiming that we had a quick meeting upstairs. We went back to the porch twenty minutes later, and August and Reese were laughing together, clearly new friends. Reese stayed for another hour, the four of us talking about anything except God. We relayed stories to August about our McDonald's escapades, about the labor that went into cooking one of those new

Angus burgers and the heated arguments I was having with senior citizens over the one-cent price increase of their senior coffees.

The sun was setting as Reese left. He had plans at a dance club that night and wanted to shower the McDonald's smell off his body beforehand. He walked off the porch and August went inside. Maggie and I followed him as the door swung shut behind us.

"How did it go?" Maggie and I asked. "What did you talk about? Did you share the gospel? Was he receptive? Where does he fall on the spiritual scale? What should our next steps be?"

August turned around to face our inquiring eyes. "We just talked about normal stuff. Like, the weird people we see on the beach."

I then realized how unprepared we all were for a vertical like Reese, how none of us could conceptualize God's issues with who he was. It was a hole in the core of our marketing: the exposed nerve endings of our emotions, rendering us speechless about the train we had been taught was hurtling toward him.

Maggie and I drove to work the next day, like usual, the sun rising above the shoreline.

Unlike usual, we spoke.

"What should we do about Reese?" she asked, hoarse, drained. "About any of them?"

"Pray," I answered. "Tell them that we love God. Then pray that God will reveal his chosen ones."

Maggie nodded, and in that moment, I understood what Calvinism was for. It was a theological argument that took the pressure off us as evangelizers, relieving us of the responsibility to ultimately convert people. If God had chosen Reese or any of the grill workers before time, he'd save them at some point—regardless of anything we did. God was merely inviting us into the process of saving, an honor in itself. To be a part of it, all we had to do was talk about him and pray.

*

I find prayer very difficult now, because I am scared of what will meet me if I dare to reach up. Will it be the God who chose damnation in hell for a subset of his creations, who claimed to love them yet predestined their eternal suffering? Or will it be another God entirely, one who gave us free will because he trusted us to recognize the beauty of his love? Will I think I'm reaching up to one but end up touching the other? Or will it be something else entirely? Just air?

After evangelicalism, I want to see everything. I want to see the webs that are woven around our minds, intentions planted by people other than ourselves. I want to see the pressures and the chaos and the pain that led to our peace, the tears we shed before we learned how to live with our questions. I want to see the details of the marketing plans. I want to see the verticals, so I can know if I'm the target audience.

13.

Before evangelical Christianity, I wasn't good at staying in the lane designated for me by my gender. I sometimes drove right over the solid line into oncoming traffic, because there seemed to be so much more freedom in the lives of men.

For example, in junior high, sick of not having a boyfriend, I decided to take matters into my own hands and become the pursuer instead of waiting around to be pursued. I began near-stalking a boy with a stylish, spiky haircut named Charlie. By the time Charlie arrived in the morning, I'd be leaning against his locker, hugging my books to my chest. "Hey," I'd say.

He wouldn't say anything back.

"Um, I said hi."

He'd rifle through his locker in silence.

"You going to be at the dance next Friday? I hear you take woodshop on Mondays. Don't you think Mr. Wilson looks like a goat?"

Nothing I said brought a sound out of Charlie. Instead, his cheeks turned red. *How cute*, I thought. *He must really like me! I bet this is his first time getting attention from a girl.* In all honesty, I think Charlie was a little scared, but I couldn't see his feelings past my own iron will.

"Why won't you talk to me?" I asked in an attempt to let

him know that his bashful demeanor was causing me emotional turmoil.

As he walked away, I followed him down the stairs and outside. "See you tomorrow?" I asked. He climbed onto the bus, without even a glance back as the door closed behind him.

I didn't realize at first how much stricter gender roles were within evangelical Christianity. Our campus Cru ministry was a women-led operation, started by Tara, developed further by Cate, and staffed by Hannah, Leigh, and me. Innocently, I assumed that a women-led Christian organization was perfectly normal—until Hannah's boyfriend Noah began to attend our Bible studies.

Noah had met Hannah while working the sign-in table at one of our regional Cru meetings. He went to another college in New Jersey and lived over an hour away. Like a belligerent rooster, he'd peck his way into conversations. He wanted to have the first word at dawn, and his demeanor at Bible study made me realize that he saw the women around him as hens. As Cate taught, Noah would lean back, pen behind his ear, hands folded over his chest. He'd stroke the small flap of hair on his chin and stare at her, not once flipping to the Bible verses we were focusing on. No notes, no questions, no participation beyond his presence.

"I'm not a fan of Noah," Cate confided to me after he pulled her aside at the end of one of the Bible studies he attended.

"What did he say?" I asked.

"He told me that he could run our Bible study better and that we need more men in leadership."

"Who does this guy think he is?"

"I mean, he's not wrong," Cate said. "But I can't come up with what I don't have! We're working this way out of necessity."

I had gathered that this was somehow part of the rules, but did Cate really think this oaf's presence would somehow enhance our movement, just because he was a man? "Do you honestly believe he could do a better job than you?" I asked.

"It's not about *better*," Cate said. "Men are ordained to lead. It's just the way God works."

As I was learning, the way God worked meant that there were quite a few things godly, biblical woman could not do.

They could not, for example, be pastors. The Bible was clear on the matter. In 1 Timothy 2:12, Paul writes, "I do not permit a woman to teach or to exercise authority over a man; rather, she is to remain quiet." Women could teach or exercise authority over children or other women, but not over men. None of the churches I attended let women do more than teach Sunday school, make announcements, or maybe read scripture into a microphone.

Women also weren't allowed to ask men out on dates. When it came to the precarious waters of courtship, we were not allowed to step foot in the stream first. There was no specific biblical precedent about this, but I was told that it was based on the way men were wired. "Men want to pursue women," Michelle, my Cru discipler, said. "They're born to hunt. If you ask him out, you'll be robbing him of his role." I was not supposed to be focusing on men, anyway; while I was single, God was the one who I should be looking to for love. And besides, it made sense to wait on a man to ask me out, because his bravery in the act would prove that he'd be capable of leading me in marriage.

Which brings me to another thing women weren't allowed to do: be anything but submissive in marriage. In Ephesians 5:22–23, Paul says, "Wives, submit to your own husbands, as to the Lord. For the husband is head of the wife even as Christ is head of the church." This sounded distinctly unequal to me, and I felt offended, even angry, that God would demand such a thing. But I was told that submission didn't mean inequality. My relationship with my husband would reflect the care that Christ bestowed upon the church. The man played the role of Christ and would act as the loving head of our household. He wouldn't make me do anything I didn't want to do—he would just make all the final decisions.

To aid me in wrapping my mind around this, I was told that God commanded these things due to the natural demeanor of each gender. Women, Cru said, were born wanting control and power, as shown by the way Eve was easily tempted by Satan and approached Adam with the apple. Therefore, God relinquished our control to grow us, to help us develop beyond the comfort that came with having authority over situations. Men, on the other hand, were not born wanting control and power, as shown by the way they all seemed to shirk responsibility in relationships and around the house. God, as a result, bestowed control upon them to aid them in their lifelong quest of becoming responsible adults.

These restrictions sat in the back of my head and gnawed away at my trust in God. I'd confess this to Cate, and she'd ask me why I hated men.

"I just don't understand why we have to take a back seat to them," I'd say.

"It's not a back seat. It's a seat right beside them! Can't you trust God with this?"

But it was hard to trust God about Hannah's relationship with Noah.

A friend of ours told me what she saw happen between them on a car ride. "He was driving, and she was in the passenger's seat. He wouldn't stop touching her leg. She kept asking him to stop, and he wouldn't, and then she'd push his hand away and he'd squeeze harder."

"How do you know he squeezed harder?" I asked.

"Because she yelled 'Stop, that hurts!'"

Though she commuted from her parents' house, Hannah slept over in my dorm once a week because she had an early class. I had one day a week to talk to her about this, one day a week to convince her that she should end this relationship.

I learned that my powers of persuasion were less developed than I realized.

"He just gets excited sometimes," Hannah said of the car-ride squeezing.

"Excited enough to physically hurt you?"

"He didn't mean to hurt me. He's a guy! He's got big hands."

"Plenty of guys have big hands and don't hurt their girlfriends with them."

"We've talked about it, okay? He promises to be gentler."

I told her that Noah didn't behave like a godly man, didn't show grace or patience or any of the virtues we were supposed to look for in a future husband. She told me that nobody was perfect, and she saw other sides of him—gentleness and tenderness, a potential to turn into that man. They had talked about getting married, and she was waiting for him to propose.

"Hannah, you don't have to marry this guy. You really don't have to do this."

"I know. I just don't want to start over."

I turned to Cate, queen of logic, to see if further sense could be talked into Hannah. I had spent all my resources, every last late-night talk, trying to tell Hannah something she didn't want to hear.

"Oh, I've talked to her, too," Cate said. "Believe me, I have."

Cate told me that there was hope as long as they weren't married, that for the days leading up to their wedding, we could try to convince Hannah not to do it.

"What about after, though? What do we do if she goes through with it?"

"Then our role is to keep them together."

It was nonsensical to me, the notion that abuse of any kind should be tolerated in a marriage, but I had already learned that divorce was reprehensible under any circumstances.

"What about abuse?" I asked. "What would you do if your husband hit you?"

"Well, I'd probably ask him 'What's up with that?'" Cate responded.

I was under absolutely zero impression that an action like that would suffice, but I decided to table the beef I had with this teaching and deal with it later.

✷

In the early weeks of Summer Project, the women were spoken to exclusively by the male staff leaders. We were told to ask them anything we wanted about the way their gender thought, or felt, or viewed the world. "Get your curiosity out," Naomi, the woman who had grilled me about my porn-viewing habits over the phone, said with a wry smile.

We filed in to the pews of a church as the six male staff leaders sat up by the pulpit, and raised our hands cautiously to ask questions about dating. "Are guys afraid of asking us out?" Yes, but it was their job. "Will they get the guts to do it?" Sure, if you're the right girl.

I whispered to Cam and Jennifer, "Watch this." I raised my hand and shouted, "What do you want from us?"

The women in the pews laughed at this question that had been on all our minds, but the head male staff member looked at me dourly from across the room. "Respect," he answered.

Then on to the next question.

I felt deflated, like a broken balloon. I closed my eyes and thought, *There's something wrong with me. I don't know why I hate men.*

During women's time, however, Naomi taught us something new. She was talking about how the differences between the God-ordained roles of men and women had nothing to do with equality. She said that God had created us differently, and the role of women was biblically honorable. "Does anyone know what the word *ezer* means?" she asked.

No one had any idea, because she was speaking ancient Hebrew.

According to Naomi, the English translation of *ezer* was "helpmeet," and it was used in the book of Genesis to describe the Holy Spirit and Eve: "The same word that was used to describe the Holy Spirit, the most powerful force of the Godhead, was used to describe women! The very *first* woman!"

I was mystified. Could it be that women were as wonderful in God's eyes as the Holy Spirit?

In a way, it was a relief to believe that I was supposed to relax and let God handle everything. "You get the easier job!" Naomi used to say about dating. "You don't have to sweat fearing you'll be rejected!" I wasn't afraid of rejection, as I felt strong enough to lift my head off the ground if I was knocked down by a no. But I also felt like the world wanted me to stay in my role, to ask fewer questions and be okay with fewer answers. At thirteen, I had stepped out of my role and tried to pursue Charlie. It was unacceptable behavior, and even the nonbelievers around me had said as much at the time. ("*You're* going after *him*?" one girl asked. "No wonder he's running away from you.")

Pursuit, I now saw, belonged to men. That was their God-given role. I had been stupid, and young, and sinful, to think that it was appropriate to pursue Charlie. I had stepped out of God's order and paid the price in humiliation. My role was to be the person God wanted me to be—which was an obedient woman who was quiet of heart. I was not to cause a fuss or harvest anger in my bones against biblical teachings. I was to line up against a wall and let a man pick me. After that, during marriage, he would make the decisions. It would be fine. He would take my opinion into account. He wouldn't make me do anything I didn't want to do.

Now, as a single woman, my husband was God, and my duty as a good wife was to support him in what he wanted, what he did. But I'm not sure God and I ever got ourselves to the wedding altar. I don't think we exchanged rings. I promised him forever before I understood forever, before the gravity of a walk down an aisle fully hit me. We were not married, despite the analogies I was given. We were courting, I think—in a serious relationship. I played the role, for seven years, of God's girlfriend, and I promised to marry him no matter how much he hurt me.

*

On the last day of Summer Project, August asked me to take a walk to the beach. I thought he was going to tell me he'd pursue me from a distance, ask me what I needed to feel wanted from several states away.

We walked to the stairs in front of the sand, and sat at the top, looming over footprints and grass patches.

"I think Barbara has been telling you some things that aren't good," he said. He explained that she had begun prophesying to him about me. She told him that we were meant to be together but that he had a choice in the matter. He realized that she was most likely saying similar things to me and getting my hopes up about something he had no intention of doing.

"She's trying to play matchmaker," he said, "but there's nothing she's telling us that's rooted in biblical truth." He went on about his distaste for long-distance relationships, how he didn't want to spend time trying to figure out how to make one work. He told me that we could wait and see what happened, could talk until he graduated college, but even then, it would be several years until we could date. "Besides," he said, "you're going to grad school. You have your life figured out. I don't, and I need someone to go along with me while I do."

I understood, in that moment, what Barbara had been saying about giving up my dreams in order to be with August. But she was wrong; I didn't even get to choose to give them up. My goals, my dreams, my future—August had already decided those for me. He wanted to be with someone who would follow him where he went, wanted a blank slate of a woman on whom he could write the role he wanted her to play. I was not that woman. I couldn't be that woman. My entire being, the fiber of it, wouldn't allow me to be that woman.

"You okay?" August asked.

"Yeah. Yeah, I am."

A hundred questions sat waiting to launch in the core of my stomach, but I did not release any of them. August had told me that he didn't want to pursue me, didn't want to be with me, for reasons outside of my control. Asking any questions would turn me into a person pursuing him. I needed to stay silent, because questioning him was not my role.

Sitting there on the beach with him that last time, I began poring through every word that Barbara had ever said to me, trying to separate her claims of prophecy from my own false hopes. I watched the ocean waves reach toward the shore as August closed our conversation in prayer, asking God to protect our hearts for our future spouses, and as he did, I remembered telling Barbara about the abusive relationship between Hannah and Noah—asking for her advice, her wisdom.

"Oh, my husband hit me once!" she had said. "We went immediately to our pastor, who told him that was unacceptable."

"And did it work?" I asked. "Has he hit you since?"

"Not once! See what happens when you let the Lord handle it?"

14.

I moved to New York City for graduate school in August 2009, heartsick but hopeful that the city would heal me. My parents drove me from Massachusetts, a trailer in tow. During the four-hour trip, I kicked off my flip flops and sat, legs crossed, on the car seat, wearing my blue Live Free or Die T-shirt from Summer Project. The world I knew passed by in green. I told myself that living in the city would be a restorative experience, like traveling to another country, something to give me perspective after I had been rejected by August. It was time to start over. Maybe New York would show me how.

I had been to Manhattan before, but only for spans of a few hours, trips in and out. In college, I occasionally ventured in for museum visits, one time pouring wine at a theater benefit. It was foreign territory to me, and even though I'd gotten into The New School several months ago, I'd never taken a moment to study street maps or subway lines. I had been too busy working at McDonald's, trying to convert nonbelievers, and, I had mistakenly thought, finding my future husband.

We arrived at my dorm building, located in the Financial District, which I had chosen over Craigslist housing because the thought of internet roommates scared the Holy Spirit out of me. The RAs directed me to my quarters on the fourteenth floor, and my father and I took the elevator with a hand truck he'd made himself, onto which he had somehow bungee-corded eight boxes. "Looks like your roommate's already here," he said. One of the beds was made up with sheets and a comforter.

My parents helped me unpack and ate dinner with me, then left, hugging me and saying that they'd be back next month. I hoped I'd be a successful New York City woman by then, blowing people away with my fashion sense and newfound self-confidence, on my way to an unstoppable future. I wanted my Facebook picture to show me at a fancy party with a cocktail in hand, my short hair in ringlets, a well-fitting dress sparkling as I looked over my shoulder. I wanted to meet people who would invite me to that kind of fancy party. People so glamorous that I'd forget all about August.

What constituted success had seemed so much simpler before I arrived in New York. During Summer Project, we kept two tally boards in the kitchen of the White Gull—one for all the people we shared the gospel with, another for those who had accepted Jesus through us. At the end of each week, we would send the numbers off to headquarters to be included with stats from all the Summer Projects around the world. A personal relationship with Jesus was quantifiable. Success, in God's eyes, hinged on evangelism.

Now that God had accepted me into his kingdom, success took on a new meaning, one just as rigid, but somehow more achievable. I was no longer alone in my fight for success, no longer dependent on the opinions of my parents to feel like I was on the right path. I now had entire communities and churches joining me in my dream, uncountable others who wanted to see God's vision come to life in the most influential city in the world—the equivalent of Jesus's Rome. But first, I needed to find out who those people were around me.

✷

My roommate, Eleanor, was the first, most obvious person for me to share the gospel with. We had met on move-in day, when her parents were helping her unpack. They were a quiet, sophisticated-seeming family from the Midwest. Her father offered me some Guinness. I was twenty-one, but I hadn't thought of drinking alcohol for several months, as consuming it was against Project rules. Still, I let him pour me some and drank the fizzy, bitter cream as I talked to Eleanor. She was so adult, with her porcelain skin, sophisticated glasses, and shaggy Sally-Bowles-in-*Cabaret* hair. She intimidated me, but I reminded myself that I could do all things through Christ—even earn the trust of someone who I could already tell trusted rarely.

After her parents went to their hotel, Eleanor and I chatted a little more and then she went to bed. I wanted to be excited about my future, but instead fell asleep with the discomfort of sleeping in a new bedroom with a stranger.

When I woke up, I called Jennifer, my married Project roommate, to tell her how lonely I was.

"You know how close I live to the city, right?" she said. "Literally a ten-minute bus ride through the tunnel." I thus spent my first month in New York leaving Eleanor on weekends and taking a bus to more familiar faces in New Jersey.

When classes started up, I didn't do any better at making friends. My classmates seemed pompous in their flannel and tattoos. Their writing was all about meaningless sex and the futility of marriage—miles away from glorifying Jesus. They worshiped in the wrong places, idolizing Proust and Murakami instead of, say, the words God had written through the apostle Peter. I couldn't swallow what I was being fed, because what I had eaten on Project had been so different—friendship and community and biblically centered love, not narcissism and sex-obsession and the meat of carnal desires.

I talked to God. *I don't know how to do what you want me to do here.*

✷

I found a church within my first month in the city, one that I had heard of from a woman I met at a park while babysitting a nine-month-old. She had moved to New York for dance, but was now nursing a knee injury and picking up babysitting jobs through people she met at church.

My ears sprang. "What's your church called?" I asked.

"Hope," she said. "Hope Church NYC. It's for artists."

"An artist church. Cool. Is it Christian, or something else?"

"Oh, definitely Christian. We're followers of Christ."

Upon further research, I discovered that this church was legit evangelical, part of Mark Driscoll's Acts 29 church-planting network. I showed up at the Upper West Side address the next Sunday in my best tan capris, hair in a bun with sunglasses atop my head. It didn't look like a church from the outside—more like an apartment building with the door ajar, a sign outside that said "Hope meets upstairs." I climbed a flight of circular stairs to a lobby full of female greeters. They wore nice jeans and high heels and long chain necklaces as they handed me smooth paper bulletins. This, I realized, was what New York City Christian ladies looked like.

I went into the service area, which looked like a small dinner theater. Red curtains lined the stage, and long tables extended from the walls. I sat in the middle of one of the tables, wanting to be accessible in case anyone decided to befriend me. I stood as the room darkened, the worship leaders taking the stage.

A blonde woman in stiletto boots donned a guitar, and in a raspy, soulful voice, sang a tune about God she had written herself. The stylish people all around me lifted their hands up in praise, closing their eyes and swaying as the Holy Spirit moved them. I felt out of place in this spiritual family, an outsider looking in at the world of urban Christian culture.

After worship, a pastor named Luke took the stage. In his baggy suit pants and oversize corduroy jacket, he was perhaps the only person besides me who didn't look like he had walked out of a fashion catalogue. He delivered an intellectually and emotionally rigorous sermon. I liked his style. He was like an awkward professor dad, the kind who might wear a fanny pack, handing knowledge down from the pulpit and telling us not to spend it all at the arcade.

I approached him as soon as the service was finished and told him that I was hardcore into ministry and was there to help God convert the entire city.

"How wonderful that you're so passionate for the Lord!" he said, a faint drawl emerging in his voice. "We've only been around a year, and we need people like you!"

He told me about the church's beginnings—he was friends with *the* Pastor Tim Keller (August's favorite writer!) of Redeemer Presbyterian Church in Manhattan (the church August always wanted to visit!), who had coached him through moving to New York to plant a church. He'd been an atheist musician in a former life, before God got ahold of him, and was passionate about cultivating a space for fellow artists to explore their creativity and what it could mean for Jesus. Artists of all kinds, and at all stages in their professional lives, went here—from painters still in school to directors putting out their first films, and even Grammy winners, like the worship leader, who had written a hit song for Jennifer Lopez.

If only August could see me now, rubbing elbows with a songwriter for JLo! All my friends from Project would be so impressed. I was making some serious moves to gain influence for the Lord!

At the end of our conversation, Pastor Luke told me that he hoped to see me again next Sunday. "I'm serious. We need someone like you."

✷

In addition to church, I was also interested in establishing a Cru chapter at The New School. I found an email address for a man who led the Campus Crusade for Christ movement in NYC, and sent him a message. He emailed back to set up a meeting at the NYC Metro Cru offices for later that week. When I arrived, he was eating spinach out of a bowl and made a weird joke about Popeye and growing himself "little muscles." I laughed out of courtesy and sat down, eager to discuss starting a Cru movement at my school.

"We've been trying to get a movement going there for a long time," he said. "Difficult, though. Staff members haven't had much luck sharing the gospel."

I learned that movements at colleges started in one of two ways: Either Cru staff members went to campus and shared tract booklets with the students, or the students who were already believers reached out to Cru and did the gospel sharing themselves. I, of course, fell into the latter category.

"What if there are other believers on campus?" I asked. "What if I just need to find them?"

"That's very possible."

"But how can I do that?"

"The old-fashioned way. Flyers!"

I went back to my dorm room and designed flyers, the lost-dog type with a fringe of tear-off phone numbers at the bottom. I was looking to target true-blue believers, not people who were trying on a faith, so I chose the headline LOOKING FOR CHRISTIAN COMMUNITY AT THE NEW SCHOOL? TEXT BETH AND JOIN A BIBLE STUDY! I was not much of an art director, but I managed to find a picture of a Bible on Google, which I copied and pasted to the center of the flyer. I printed out forty flyers in the library and taped them to as many walls as I could around the school.

One person texted back, a nice girl who I met up with and tried to sell on doing initiative evangelism with me. She said, "No thanks, but let me know when you've got a Bible study going!" No other texts came. When I checked the flyers after a week, only one phone number had been torn off.

Frustrated, but not broken, I decided to dive into church more. After all, Cate always said that Cru was merely a substitute for the community I was supposed to receive there. I decided that I could be doing more to connect with people. I *needed* to be doing more.

I talked to Pastor Luke, and he told me to join a women's Bible study.

"There's one at Amy's house!" he said, beckoning to a blonde women who didn't talk much. She stood next to Pastor Luke, meek and tall, a half-eaten donut hole in her hand, and said in a crackling voice, "Would you like to join?"

"Yes!" I exclaimed.

I showed up at Bible study later that week, leather-bound Bible in hand, and Amy offered me a glass of wine. Alcohol seemed to be a part of everything in New York. I decided to take a glass, shame-free—hey, this was Bible study! Other women arrived in slim-fitting dresses and costume jewelry. I was prepared to blend in this time: flared jeans with little wedge heels, a long blue shirt with a gold chain belt around my hips. I had been studying.

On Summer Project, Bible study was rigorous. We dug in, parsing out the verses, Googling the original meanings of Hebrew and Greek words. NYC Bible study, on the other hand, was light and airy. We read the verses and meditated on them gently. No one was trying to be a theologian here.

When I left, I felt like I was on my way to making friends. I convinced myself that if I had been looking in from the outside, I would have seemed like one of them—a New York City Christian lady, classy in Jesus. I went home and friended the women on the Facebook group.

The following weekend, I saw Facebook pictures of them dancing with cute cocktails at a bar. It was Amy's birthday. They had all gone out. I hadn't been invited.

I sat back in my chair and felt the rejection of my childhood. These women may have been my sisters in Christ, but I felt like I wasn't sophisticated enough, not adult enough, not *something* enough to get an invitation into their circle.

I don't know how to live here, I thought.

✷

Following Christ, I thought, was supposed to alleviate this loneliness, this ache of being without people. I had entered the evangelical movement with the promise of a worldwide family, brothers and sisters everywhere. But in New York, people were busy. They were adults. They already had their friends. And it felt clear to me that I wasn't adult enough to be their friend yet.

I felt that I needed to grow, past Campus Crusade, past college dorms and unusable kitchens, into the world of bars and nights out and a glass of wine before bed. I needed to stop trying to create the life I used to have and focus on the one I had now. *But what is my life now?* I asked God as I walked down streets, into subways and out of them, down more streets, into buildings. Whatever it was, it felt like less than the life I had before.

My first visit to New York had been at the age of seventeen, on a day-long chorus field trip. Morgan and I had bought books at a Barnes and Noble near Times Square ("a bookstore in New York City!") and ate at Sbarro's ("a restaurant in New York City!"). We fantasized about living here someday when we were rich and famous, Morgan a renowned jazz singer, I a published author. It felt like the greatest successes of our lives were at hand, like in tasting that Sbarro's, we were taking preliminary bites of glory. All of the hard-earned successes we had garnered thus far in our small town, our concert solos and lead roles and fights for student council recognition, were nothing compared to what we'd experience once we stepped into the real world.

Throughout my first year in the city, that day with Morgan ran through my head. Had my desire to be famous been selfish, narcissistic? Was it bad that I still wanted to be famous now? Could I make it about God?

I replayed my last moment on the beach with August, trying to justify my submissiveness, the way I showed no anger and asked no questions. I was angry now, angry enough to scream, at the idea that he didn't want me because my future was too vibrant, too independent of him. He was a man set apart by God, and I wasn't allowed to dim his light with my own. It made me want to shine even brighter, so bright he couldn't escape me. I wanted to be on his TV screen, showing him what he was missing, showing him that with me, he could have been a star.

Then August told me he'd be visiting New York City with his college ministry and suggested I meet him and some of his friends for dinner. We hadn't spoken much since the end of Summer Project. He had wanted to remain friends from afar, but my female friends warned me against it, advising me to guard my heart. I agreed to see him, feeling nervous. I wanted to come off as a seasoned New Yorker, not the naïve beach girl he'd rejected.

His ministry was staying at a hostel in Harlem, and I met him there, along with three of his friends. We spent the rest of our time on an adventure to Times Square and Battery Park. I took them to my favorite dessert place on Bleecker Street, and to the record store next door. I told August I was getting into the band Arcade Fire, and he bought me one of their CDs. There was no way, I thought, that he wasn't in love with me. No Christian man who abstained from even brushing up against a girl when he walked by would purchase her a CD if he didn't mean something by it, at least subconsciously.

My visions of us on subway platforms in scarves and peacoats reemerged. I could introduce him to my pastor's dear friend Tim Keller, and we could sit on an elite board at Keller's church and work tirelessly, side by side, to bring Christ to the city. We could be a Christian power couple!

Two months later, August called and left a voicemail. "It's me. Call back when you have a chance." I did, but he didn't pick up, nor did he return my call.

A month after that, I saw that he had updated his Facebook profile. *In a relationship,* it said.

15.

I met Will in a writing class during my second semester of grad school. On the first day of class, it seemed like he already knew everyone, saying hello to the other students as they put their bags down, striking up easy conversations. I had spent the semester before making a total of zero friends—just a few acquaintances who I smiled at as they seemed to vaguely recognize me in the halls. *Who is this social wizard?* I thought, discomfited by Will's own comfort. The writers surrounding us were the least forthcoming people I had encountered, yet here this guy was dragging joy out of their stoic, Jack Kerouac exteriors.

I went home that night and looked him up on Facebook. His profile picture showed him in a cardigan and a striped scarf, holding a beer stein up to the camera as if saying cheers to the whole world. It screamed, *Relax and have fun*, but my life before New York hadn't included biergartens, or beer, or really any recreational drinking that involved anything but milkshakes or Tampico. I didn't know how to fit into that world, or if there was even any space in it for someone like me.

As the semester went on, I began to realize that Will was silent once class started and we began to dig into the depths of each other's writing. He had little to add that didn't echo what the person before him said, and I recognized an insecurity that crackled through the air as he spoke, a subtext that whispered, *I hope they don't think I'm a fraud.* Was Will just as unsure of himself as I was? Just as afraid of ending up alone? Just as desperate to discover the secret of adulthood, to grow into a respectable person surrounded by respectable friends?

One day, he submitted a nonfiction piece for workshop via email, the accompanying message a self-deprecating joke: "I hope you like my ramblings about growing up in an evangelical church!" *Evangelical?* I thought. *Does Will know Christ?* I pored over his essay and came out the other end astounded. This man had a solid spiritual foundation! He had wandered away from his childhood church because of the damnation-filled way the pastors spoke from the pulpit about homosexuality, but that was small potatoes. There were plenty of evangelical churches in New York City that approached those views in a gentle way, that purposely didn't preach about them and saved the conversations instead for coffee-shop meetings in which the pastor would kindly, and convincingly, wade with the questioner through the biblical precedents—my church being one of them.

Invite him, I felt God say inside of me. Perhaps, like Esther in the Bible, I had been placed here for Will.

I printed his essay and wrote a note on the last page about the narrative structure and how much I enjoyed his writing style. I gave him some notes about areas I thought he could improve, and then added a personal message in the last sentence: *Oh, and by the way, I'm a Christian and totally get the gripes you had with your church. I go to a church on the Upper West Side that doesn't talk about homosexuality like that. You should join me sometime—I think you'd really like it!* I asked God to help this action bear fruit.

The next week, he stopped me on the sidewalk as I left after class.

"Hey!" he said. "I read your note. Tell me more about this church."

✺

After I found out that August had a girlfriend, I barely ate for a week, throwing up what I did consume until small red dots appeared underneath my eyes. This debilitating display of emotionality over was embarrassing, over, as Cate would point out on the phone, "just a man." I was ashamed about being so sad, for feeling like the hope had been siphoned out of me, and for giving my roommate Eleanor such a pitiful illustration of what it looked like to let God take care of my heart. She wasn't seeing me at my best, at my most fulfilled in him. I was relying on anything but him to satiate my emotional needs. I saw a quote floating around on the internet: "A woman's heart should be so hidden in Christ that a man needs to seek him to find her." I wanted to hide myself in Jesus and gain that level of spiritual maturity, and then blossom until people like Eleanor could see how much better off I was for his presence.

From what I gauged during our spiritual conversations, Eleanor was a high seven on the spiritual survey scale in terms of her desire to know the real, living God. She was inquisitive about my beliefs and receptive when I explained them, no matter how extreme or, I feared, offensive-seeming they were.

"Do you think I'm going to hell?" she asked, when I told her that I thought belief in Jesus Christ was the only way to heaven.

"I would never say that," I told her. "I would never judge you like that. God knows your heart, and I believe that he's in control." I sidestepped the issues the way Cru and Cate had taught me to, keeping my eye on the goal of getting Eleanor to church, of introducing her into a community where she could learn comfortably about Christ. In addition to Will, an influx of people our age had started showing up at the church, and we filled our Sundays with after-church brunches, our Wednesdays with Bible studies and Shake Shack. It was the perfect time to get Eleanor ensconced in this growing group of church friends.

As it turned out, bringing Eleanor to church for the first time took no convincing. I asked her to come, and it was as if she had been waiting by the mailbox of our friendship for an invitation. "Sure," she said. "I've been meaning to check it out."

She sat next to me that Sunday and stood as we sang, inquisitively regarding the lyrics projected on the screen. My peripheral prayers were on her the whole time, thrumming through Pastor Luke's words as he preached. *Help her find this intellectually stimulating. Help this make her think about existence in a new way. Help this morning be her first step toward you, Lord, toward the greatest, most fulfilling relationship of her life.*

After the service, Eleanor and I took the subway home, and we talked about the message, the music, the people. "I didn't expect it to be so thought provoking," she said about the sermon. "It was like philosophy class."

Hope welled in my chest once more—a slow, steady hope that felt like a gift. Seeds were planted. A good impression was made. The Holy Spirit had made his entrance.

✷

Will and I stood outside Café Loup in the fall of 2010, at the beginning of our second year in the MFA program. It was the watering hole where we'd congregate with our fellow students before and after class—a historical place, I was told, an old Greenwich Village haunt that was once a meetup for famous writers like William S. Burroughs. It was also where Will and I hoped to plant the seeds of fundamentalist evangelical conversion in our friends. He had been so enthusiastic since I introduced him to the church, there before I arrived the first morning I invited him, bouncing to the music, fists pumping in the air. It seemed clear that he had outgrown the church of his childhood and needed a change like this to continue his spiritual journey. I was glad that

I had listened to God about writing that note on the back of his essay. Finally, something I had done was spiritually paying off.

The Café Loup initiative was the result of conversations I had been having with Pastor Luke for quite some time. We began to formalize it once Will entered the picture, as his presence in my life opened up a slew of social doors. Each friend Will made quickly became a friend of mine, and Pastor Luke saw the same opportunity I did—that of bringing Jesus to the lives of the emerging writers in the MFA program. Instead of trying to bring these wild, liberal-minded New Yorkers to church, we'd bring church to them. We'd focus first on strengthening our friendships individually, and then we'd develop a series of one-on-one weekly dinners for those who seemed spiritually pliable, snowballing our conversations slowly into a light Bible study. We'd then evaluate where people were on the spiritual spectrum, inviting those who we deemed ready to meet with Pastor Luke. Our friends were on an assembly line, and they didn't even know it.

We were particularly focused on an unruly band of poets we found ourselves hanging out with until the wee hours of the morning. It was a bit unusual, two straitlaced prose writers in this reckless world of poets, but we loved them. We went everywhere with them—to every reading, party, and concert—with the sole purpose of helping Jesus save them all.

That night outside of Café Loup, Will was telling me about his meeting the next morning with the executive pastor of our church, who Will wanted to be discipled by.

Will kept talking as I looked at my phone, half-listening as I read an email about a babysitting job I had the next day. The words he said blurred as my attention divided, and then I heard it.

" . . . boyfriend or best friend."

I looked up. "What?"

"I said, I mean, I could be your boyfriend or your best friend."

There it was, the thing I had been afraid of—that perhaps

Will hadn't attended church with me out of an earnest desire to know God and had instead come along because of the potential for romance. It was a fear I didn't want to acknowledge because this was a friendship I needed, one that brought me a sense of happiness and belonging that I couldn't replicate, akin to the concept of soulmates. I couldn't lose him.

"Best friend," I said. "Only best friend."

I looked at the street across from us, lights beaming dim in the windows as people walked quickly past. The air was chilled.

"And if you can't handle that," I continued, "we don't need to be friends."

"No! No, I can handle that," he said. "I'm on the same page. Yeah, let's be best friends."

That was how a woman of God should act. I was transparent with my intentions, direct in my response. I cleared away the confusion and let him know exactly where our relationship stood in the realm of my emotions. If God meant for Will to keep coming to church regardless of my feelings for him, he would.

And he did. Will came to church every Sunday, devoting himself to the worship band with his multi-instrumental talents. He took up an unofficial greeting post and welcomed new faces, digging his way into their hearts with a self-deprecating candidness. He became a fixture of sorts: hipster Will in his cardigans and thick-rimmed glasses, the one person at church you needed to be friends with if you wanted to have a fun, full life in the city.

And I, of all people, got to be his best friend.

Together, Will and I crossed the thresholds of the spiritual and the secular, staying up late on Saturday nights with our writer friends at bars. We drank IPAs and went to readings and traveled to other states, spending raucous three-day weekends with the poets in Chicago and Washington, DC. In a hotel room one night, I heard one of the poets whispering with Will in a corner.

"I'm receptive to your beliefs, you know," she said. "I've always been interested in God. I think writing poetry is like speaking in tongues."

"I just jumped back on the bandwagon," he said. "But I believe stronger now than I did before."

There he was, sharing his faith at two in the morning, doing the type of thing that I was trained for years to do but doing it, somehow, far more organically than I ever could. I was proud of him, and my body breathed deeply in bed, resting in a way that it hadn't since my first morning in the city. It was such a relief to no longer be the only Christian in a room, to have a partner who I could work with to make our God known in a city-sized sea of nonbelievers.

✷

My parents had not visited me on a Sunday since I moved to the city, always electing to come on Saturdays instead. When they, at last, decided that a Sunday worked best for them, it was the end of my second year in New York. I was thriving in both ministry and general life.

"Get here by ten," I told them, "and we'll go to church together."

They sounded apprehensive, but they ultimately humored me. They were, after all, coming to see what my life was like.

I took them to my small theater church ("Wow, this is a *church*?") and introduced them to Pastor Luke, who greeted them with his characteristically warm smile. Will sat with us, chatting my parents up, making them feel welcome, like they were talking to a normal, non-brainwashed human being. The music began and a Brazilian man who regularly played with numerous well-known bands strummed a ukulele on stage, crooning about how great God was. When Pastor Luke's turn came, his sermon was characteristically heavy on earnest philosophy, talking about God and the second law of thermodynamics. "We're losing more energy than we can generate," he said. "That's where Jesus comes in. He connects us to the Father."

At the end of the service, after the band of professional volunteer musicians caused the theater to erupt in cheers for the Lord, my mother turned to me and pointed to Pastor Luke. "Now that's a man I can listen to!" she said.

When they left that day, my mother waving to me in their car's passenger-side mirror, I felt a sense of achievement. By approving of my church, praising the music and the sermon, my parents had signaled the end of my awkward spiritual teenage hood.. I clung to the hope that, finally, a piece of my God-world resonated with them.

The good news didn't stop there. Eleanor was now attending church with me about once a month. I'd informed her that the invitation to join me was always standing, that all she needed to do was be ready with me when I left. She'd surprise me by being fully showered by nine o'clock a.m. on the occasional Sunday morning, a bowl of cereal remnants in the sink, ready to go before I was.

One such morning happened to be Easter, when she walked into my room in a lilac dress and white cardigan, asking what my plans were for after the service. It was the perfect day to bring Eleanor to church, as a guest speaker that day was preaching about the Shroud of Turin—the cloth that had supposedly covered Jesus in the time between his death and resurrection. The speaker had a PhD in physics and taught at a university down south. According to Pastor Luke, he believed in a "theistic evolution," combining the truths of science with what appeared in the Bible. Eleanor had a science-based mind, and I hoped that the speaker would present the type of evidence she needed to give her life to Jesus.

Both Eleanor and I were completely entranced by the speaker, a stringy, intelligent gentleman who wore wiry spectacles and kept his feet planted in one position the entire time he spoke. He began his talk by bringing up the story of doubting Thomas, the apostle who, in John 20:24–29, couldn't believe that Jesus had been resurrected until he felt the nail marks on his hands, the wound on his side. He told us that doubting Thomas was beloved by Jesus, that empirical evidence was something God wanted to give to his children. He continued to give us his scientific opinion about the Shroud of Turin—which he had studied—saying that the image of Jesus that was burned into it could only have gotten there through the power of two atom bombs.

Eleanor sniffled during the final worship session of the service. On our way home, she told me that she was on the verge of giving her life to Jesus. "I have some more questions. But I'm almost there."

✷

Regardless of how good I was getting at sniffing out potential believers, I still needed a day job to bring in extra money. During my second year in New York, I decided to supplement my babysitting income by working retail.

I was granted employment at a store that sold all the types of shelving and storage solutions which I didn't think a person could possibly need. I was funneled into the "loss prevention" team, which meant I had to stand at the front of the store and attempt to identify thieves. This was a far more boring task than it sounds, as catching shoplifters consisted mostly of making sure people didn't take merchandise into the bathroom.

To fill my time, I wrote down notes for a story about a girl named Daisy who—unlike me—was struggling to find meaning in her life. She was also a loss-prevention employee at a store with a cultlike interest in boxes and bins, but her work experiences were far more exciting than mine. The story followed her adventures chasing a ghostly thief who evaded her in every department by disappearing into the floor. Spoiler alert: The ghost turned out to be a metaphysical force that lived in the PA system, ate loss-prevention workers, and pooped them out as the next best-selling containers.

It was a favorite in my grad school workshop class, where I brought it in three times over the course of the semester and had every page analyzed and critiqued, revising until I could practically recite each word from memory. On the last day of class, my professor encouraged me to submit it to as many journals as I could. "Someone's going to want that one," she said.

And so I did. I prayed through each submission, *God, let your will be done*, as I had written the story with an eye on him, hoping to illuminate the way nothing, not even employment, can completely fill us. I found a contest being judged by Mary Gaitskill, and I remembered a story of hers I had read a year before—"Mirrorball," in which a young man accidentally steals the soul of a woman he has a one-night stand with. It reminded me of the evangelical concept of "soul ties," which dictates that sex is a spiritual act and should be reserved for marriage because it can lead to an unbreakable soul connection between partners. I did some Googling and read that Gaitskill had converted and lapsed from evangelicalism in her early twenties. *I'll never lapse*, I thought. But the knowledge that this writer I admired had once been evangelical stuck with me, and I wondered if she'd find something kindred in the story I was about to send her way.

I was babysitting the day I got the email. "Congratulations!" it said. "Mary Gaitskill has selected your story as the first-place winner of the H.O.W. Journal Fiction Contest." The child's mother found me on the floor, phone in hand, staring at the ceiling and asking if I was dreaming. My story would be published in the journal, and I'd receive $500. It was my first time being paid for something I had written.

With that publication, I was convinced that I was following the voice of God in my life, that I was in New York City to become a writer who would share his truth with the masses. I would be like Pastor Luke, but in the literary world, making my belief in God known *along with* my vast intelligence. I would break down the stereotypes of what it meant to be evangelical, what it looked like to follow God. I would lead everyone around me toward the path that I was on. When people asked, "How did you make it?" I would say, "Jesus."

I had been taught that the ultimate evangelism tactic was "When in Rome, do as the Romans do," and I was most certainly in Rome. I was on my way to achieving a level of notoriety that I had wanted since before my walk with Christ began. I could have it all, I thought. This God. This success. I could bring the world into my world, plant seeds without being persecuted. God, I believed, was allowing me to float in calm seas he had created me for, and he was using my gifts, my willing heart, to seamlessly bring others he loved to himself.

For so long, Cru told me that God wanted to give his children better lives than they imagined. Now he was giving me just that. I couldn't let myself lose him.

16.

It's called spiritual death—the state your soul exists in if you don't believe in Jesus Christ as the only Lord and Savior. Evangelical Christians believe that anyone who has not accepted Jesus into their heart is a spiritual zombie, a teaching gleaned from Ephesians 2:1–3, when Paul speaks of those in the church of Ephesus before they knew Jesus: "And you were dead in the trespasses and sins in which you once walked, following the course of this world, following the prince of the power of the air, the spirit that is now at work in the sons of disobedience—among whom we all once lived in the passions of our flesh, carrying out the desires of the body and the mind, and were by nature children of wrath, like the rest of mankind."

Part of walking with Jesus involved not acting like a spiritual zombie, acknowledging the life inside my soul by abstaining from sex before marriage, and keeping my mind clear of any thought or fantasy that would not honor God's teachings. My writer friends who were having sex, getting drunk, smoking weed—they were doing the things that dead people did, the spiritual equivalent of eating brains. Being alive meant living in God's order, yet somehow, the longer I walked with God, the less alive I felt beside him.

In the fall of 2010, Will and I celebrated his birthday at a bar. Will said he wanted me to meet someone, presumably another nonbeliever we would try to lead to Jesus. He introduced me to a slovenly young man who looked utterly miserable in his own body. There was something almost gooey about his movements, the way he melted off the stool and oozed his hand out to shake mine.

"Hello," he said, gazing at my face as if he were looking at a star in the sky. I didn't expect to be attracted to Robert, with that victimized disposition seeping from his being, but he immediately made me feel like the most interesting woman in the world. I quickly found myself unbolting in his presence, unsealing my heart like I should have been with God. We talked for over an hour about my writing, my favorite books. His questions reached into my stories, and felt around my mind. I looked at his lips—they were plush, not slimy like I first thought. What would it be like to kiss them?

When I got up to leave, he asked what train I was taking, and I said the F. "Oh, I'm heading that way, too," he said.

When we were almost at his stop, he asked if we could grab a drink at another bar by his apartment. I said yes, thinking that being in public would keep me from doing anything I'd regret. However, instead of going to a bar, he made a beeline to the liquor store. "It's cheaper to drink at my place," he said. I wondered why the plan had changed, but I went along with it because I was suddenly self-conscious about the stringency of my belief system. I didn't want to seem like a weirdo who was afraid of entering a man's apartment.

Once inside his place, we cracked open two beers, and surveyed his bookshelf, the Nabokovs and Pynchons and Foster Wallaces. We took the books out, flipped through them, talked about what we loved in a piece of writing. He opened up about his past heartaches, the most recent being, it turned out, with a friend of mine.

"You know Alison?" he asked.

"Yeah, we had workshop together last semester."

His eyes darted diagonally from my cheeks to my mouth, as if he were searching for a reaction. "Interesting."

I looked at my phone and saw that it was two a.m.—far past the hour that it was acceptable in the Lord's eyes for me to be hanging out with a man in his apartment. "Oh, it's late!" I said, getting up to leave.

Robert stood up with me, his hands finding my face. It was a kiss I was not expecting, and before I could rest into it, I pulled away.

"No, no," I said. "Alison's my friend. I don't want to do that."

He drew close again. "It's okay." His lips pressed against mine.

I didn't know how to say no in a way that would convince Robert he needed to stop. His lips parted mine and I felt a small rage at what was happening. I had told him to stop and he didn't. My request hadn't resulted in the appropriate response. And in that moment, I stopped caring what he thought about me.

I said the one thing that I knew would repel him. "I'm an evangelical Christian!" I shouted, right into his mouth.

Robert stumbled back, finally moved by my words.

"Well, this isn't wrong," he said.

I muttered something about how it wasn't right for me, and that I needed to go home. He told me that he would walk me to the subway since it was dark, which didn't make me feel any safer but I let him do because I felt partially to blame for the situation, because what I wanted in that moment had been difficult for me to decipher—had I confused him because I was confused? I walked out of the apartment and he followed me. Instead of taking the subway, I hailed a cab.

"It was great meeting you," he said as I got in the cab. I felt a sense of regret—for myself, for him. Everything was upside down. Everything was sin.

✷

The next morning, I called Cate as soon as I woke up. Uncharacteristically, she answered.

"I was kissed last night," I said. "I think it's my fault."

I explained the circumstances, how I had gone back to his apartment, how the thought of kissing him had crossed my mind before it happened. I told her that I had told him to stop and he didn't—even though I wasn't sure in the fullness of my heart if I wanted him to stop.

"Your heart here is what matters." she said. "That's where Jesus is concerned. You weren't sure you wanted it to stop, and you should have been. You shouldn't have been in that apartment in the first place."

I was not told to focus on the way I had felt ignored when I asked Robert to stop, the small rage that had led me to push him away. Instead, I was told instead to focus on *my* sin, the sin of wanting to kiss a nonbeliever, of wanting to experience the type of connection my classmates were, of wanting to live like a child of wrath and deny my Savior. Of course Robert hadn't treated me honorably—he was a spiritual zombie who was dead in his trespasses and didn't have the ability to care for me in the ways I deserved. But I too had acted like a dead person when I walked into his apartment, lusting after the hungers of the flesh. I was better than that. I was a daughter of the King. I couldn't do something like that again.

✷

A part of trying to convert my writing friends included "doing life" with them—which meant getting involved in joint activities that would create opportunities for spiritual conversations. Because of this, I leapt at the chance to purchase a farm share with my poet friend Jack in 2011, the summer after we graduated. I'd bike up to his place once a week to get my eggs and berries and occasional tomatillos. I would find him sautéing radishes at the stove, shirtless but still wearing black shorts, black socks and black sneakers.

By this point, we'd had many conversations about his atheism, all of which made the Holy Spirit inside of me roll his eyes. Jack was unconvertable and I knew it. He was completely opposed to the supernatural, saying, "If it's not natural, it can't exist. 'Super'-natural is implausible." He told me that he didn't like the fact that I taught children's church, because "it isn't right for you to be indoctrinating young minds." Still, he was my friend, and I wanted to see him believe. I wanted to spend eternity cooking radishes with him in heaven.

On one of my egg-and-produce trips, we discussed sex before marriage. I told him my views, which I thought were quite evolved, because I had noticed during my time in the evangelical movement that men didn't get chastised for premarital sex in the same way that women did, often receiving slaps on the wrist instead of having to pray for Jesus to "restore their virginity." This was a double-standard, and I didn't think it was fair. The church, I told Jack, should come down just as hard on men.

"I don't think the church should come down hard on anyone," he said. "Guys and girls should both be free to have sex as much as they want."

I hadn't thought of that before—sexual freedom regardless of gender. Even before I converted, I was accustomed to a world in which women were labeled "sluts" or "chickenheads" because of what we did sexually with men. It wasn't much better to be called a prude or a virgin, but I'd always wanted to wait for a ring and then have sex in what I saw as a safe context.

But what would the world be like if women could be like men? What if the safety I had found inside of Christianity was not a pasture with fences, but a small cage? What if the answer was opening the gates, letting the sheep out, and allowing them to grow past their surroundings? Dangerous thoughts, questions I shouldn't be asking myself. I was supposed to believe that Jack was spiritually dead for the way he lived, but here he was in front of me, living vibrantly, partaking in relationships that seemed more liberating than anything I had experienced.

He had recently begun dating another of my poet friends, Erin, whom I had grown quite close to in my efforts to convert her. Sharing entire bottles of wine over many late-night dinners, Erin asked questions about the ins and outs of my faith, receptive to every element. I felt admired by her for exactly who I was, and it was a strange sensation to be hiding so much—my ulterior motives to convert her, to evolve her into a different person. It felt like she loved me unconditionally. How could a person who didn't know Jesus come by this so naturally? I tried to rationalize it away with teachings about the *imago dei*, the idea that we were all made in the image of God, and thus, even without becoming believers, we all have the capacity for God-like kindness.

One night, we got a bottle of sake at a nice restaurant. A stranger at a table across from us chimed in when the bottle came. "That's some really good sake!" he said, noting that he was a connoisseur. "I've gotten bottles all over the city and still haven't had anything that good. Enjoy!"

Without a moment to breathe, Erin asked for another glass. She proceeded to fill it with sake, then gave it to the man. A palpable joy swept across his face, which felt more significant than the loose inheritance of the *imago dei*—it felt like the action of Jesus himself. How could someone who didn't know Jesus love a stranger this way?

✷

During the first year after my conversion, I decided to stop swearing completely, cold turkey. Cate and I talked about what it meant to "take the Lord's name in vain," and she told me that not swearing was a way in which we could set ourselves apart as Christians. "It's a simple thing we can do to show we're different. And when people notice we're different, they may start to ask why." Essentially, not swearing was an evangelism tactic.

I didn't swear for a full three years. Not a "fuck" or a "shit" passed through my lips. To aid in my withdrawal, I began using less offensive terms in their stead, like "crap," or "darn it," or "heck." Cate told me to watch my language whenever she caught me saying "Oh my God." So "Oh my God" became "Oh my gosh."

But life in New York made me rethink my non-swearing ways. I read Samuel Beckett's *The Unnamable* in grad school, and I began to think about the functionality of language—why we speak it, our frustrations with it, the fact that it can never fully convey what we want to say. I realized that as much as I loved writing, I had so often been at a loss for words, and I remembered that saying "fuck" in my teenage years often seemed to get closer to what I meant than any other word.

With the exception of my church community, the people around me in the city swore heartily and happily—all of my friends in grad school, the neighbors who lived on my street, strangers on the subway, in coffee shops, at bars. New York, in itself, felt like a curse word, angry and excited and overwhelmed in its multiple meanings. I could easily argue that, in my new environment, swearing was an evangelism tool—one that cloaked my words in linguistic disguise, allowing me to enter new conversational spaces. When in Rome.

I told Cate about this on a weekend visit to New Jersey, the summer after I graduated with my master's degree. It was my first time hanging out with her and her husband Joseph since they'd gotten married earlier that year. They had been engaged for less than six months; the church warned about lengthy engagements and the heightened sexual temptations that came with them. She had known her new husband since they were teenagers. They had dated off and on over the years, finding their way back to each other after Cate dumped Mark ("I don't know why, but holding his hand was like holding a dead fish.")

I had liked Joseph from the first time I met him, when he came to our dorm room sophomore year and played *Lord of the Rings* Trivial Pursuit with us over three bags of Lemonheads. He was tall, bear-like, his arm span wide as he hugged Cate at the door before leaving. (I watched them from the corner of my eye—would they kiss? Why did the thought of it make my stomach ache?) He was more of an emotional being than Cate, not quite as ruled by logic, and he'd renewed his faith since they reunited. Cate confided in me privately about his now-relinquished porn addiction and how God put it in her heart to get back together with him *right* when he, unbeknownst to her, finally admitted it to a pastor. Praise Jesus!

Cate and Joseph picked me up from the train station and drove me to a house Cate's sister was renting, where we went straight into the pool. We rode pool noodles like horses in the water, sun reflecting off the padding underneath our feet, water sparkling bright blue.

"I've been thinking a lot about swearing," I said.

Cate and Joseph's interest piqued. "Oh yeah? What about it?" said Cate.

"I'm just thinking, you know, how did swears become *swears* anyway?" I told them how I'd read on the internet that words like "fuck" and "shit" originated in poor communities, in lower classes that wealthy people wanted to distinguish themselves from. "I mean, was swearing ever really about God, or was it more about class? Like, the Bible doesn't tell us, 'Thou shalt not say fuck.' How do we even know that 'fuck' is a swear?"

Joseph, now that he was married and officially the spiritual head of his wife, addressed the topic first. "I think it's about the example we're setting as believers," he said. "It's really a way to set ourselves apart, by not using language that's almost universally known as bad."

"But what makes it *bad*?" I questioned. "The fact that poor people used it? Aren't we selling our faith short if we die on a hill like that?"

Cate then entered the argument. "Well, people don't think about it like that. Most people just hear a swear and they know it's offensive."

"Not people who swear," I said. "It's like any other word to them."

The deliberations went on. They lauded the non-swearing Christian as someone who covers all their bases, making sure not to accidentally offend the ears of disapproving fellow Christians. And, they added, if we don't know how God feels about the word "fuck," it was better to simply not use it and avoid the risk of sin altogether. I didn't think their argument held much water and told them so, dunking my head underwater in dissent. I knew that I was disappointing Cate.

The next day, Cate took me to the vegetable garden of a friend from her church and encouraged me to take as many cucumbers home as I wanted. I opened my backpack and started a new conversation as my eyes traveled down the vines.

"You know, Campus Crusade didn't make it easy for me to transition to life after college," I said. "I felt lost for a long time. I was surrounded by all these amazing people, and then—they were all gone."

She stood abruptly from her kneeling position. "Well, they're working on that, you know. They've got a new program that helps people prepare for graduation."

"But it's more than that. They act like a church, but they claim they're not one." Campus Crusade itself identified as a "parachurch"—an organization that, through ministry, acts as a conduit and funnels new converts into churches around the world. My problem, I explained, was that they didn't funnel us into church communities soon enough—communities that could be lifelong sources of friendship and faith-boosting. Instead, they gave us Bible studies and monthly meetings and, most importantly, communities of believers our own age who became our best friends, the people we lived our lives with. And then, when we graduated, they wrenched it all away, as we were discouraged from attending Cru Bible studies and told to join *actual* churches, make new friends, surround ourselves with strangers.

"They fake us out," I said. "It's emotionally devastating."

Cate didn't like my analysis. She said it wasn't Cru's fault that moving to a city like New York was hard. I answered that I should have been able to move anywhere without feeling as demolished as I did. Cru made me dependent on them and then took themselves away. In teaching me to need God, they taught me to need them instead.

"You're being rebellious," Cate said. "Like a teenager. All of this. You're rebelling against your spiritual parents."

"I'm not! I'm pointing out a valid issue."

"No, you're picking apart the ones who raised you. You're tearing tiny holes wide open."

I thought about her reaction on the train ride home that day, a bag of brownies we made together sitting beside me. The sweet scent wafted upward, the chocolate still warm wrapped in tin foil. I pictured Cate in the garden, her hands curled at the fingertips, plummeting to her sides as she spoke. Twice that weekend I did not adopt her perspective. Twice I stood my ground. How long could I keep disagreeing with her? How long could I live without knowing that I had her support?

✵

I began to think more about spiritual death, because I seemed to be spiritually ill. I had probably caught it from entering Robert's apartment that night, from the kiss he delivered—I must have taken in some sort of demon. No big deal. I just needed treatment. Jesus, the Spiritual Doctor, could heal this malaise. I hauled myself to church, weary, soul coughing. I took my spiritual antibiotics, listened to Pastor Luke. I spent time with my community and took notes in my journal, faith bolstered every Sunday despite spiritual sniffles.

And then Monday began, and I woke up a little worse, my chest heavier, air harder to breathe. I had to be doing something wrong. I wasn't reading my Bible enough, wasn't taking my medicine. Sunday couldn't be my only day of treatment. I needed daily devotionals, a steady dose of the Holy Spirit to heal the core of my soul. I remembered the words of a pastor Cate and I had heard speak in college: "Why would you just eat the scraps off my table? That's all Sunday is. The scraps from my week of feeding." I needed to feed myself all week.

But my Bible was not opening, no matter what I told myself. Its pages crinkled as I switched it from bag to bag, folding over in clumps of twenty as other books pushed against it, taking up the space it was supposed to occupy. These other books eclipsed it, like clouds traveling through a dark sky, covering up a moon so its light cannot shine. The word *fuck* embedded itself in my vocabulary, and I wondered if that was the reason I felt myself turning. Was that the fatal bite of poison changing the makeup of my spiritual biology from living to dead, God's truth powering down, my organs releasing his holiness, making way for filth?

I'll get back on track, I thought. *God will save me from this*. I held on to the promise of Calvinism, the perseverance of the saints. No matter what, the theology taught, my salvation would not leave me, because I was chosen by God. I could not un-choose him.

*

In the fall of 2011, after graduating from The New School, I took on a babysitting job for a family from my church. The parents were both musicians—the father played in our worship band.

I knew that in deciding to babysit for them, I was putting myself in the middle of an odd household. They were kind but intense, going on about evil spirits, scrubbing their house for foreign statues when they found themselves in a bad mood, in case they accidentally picked up something with an evil spirit attached to it while they were on vacation. Like many evangelical Christians, they didn't celebrate Halloween, as they believed it was a celebration of evil, pagan spiritual forces. And their oldest daughter seemed like a haunted doll, her eyes glassy and plotting. Still, I was feeling weak in my faith and I needed to spend more time around godly people. This was my family in Christ, like them or not.

One rainy day, when I was warming up a glass bottle of milk in a pot on the stove for the baby, the older girl addressed me from the table where she was eating a plate of pasta: "Beth, don't look at me and don't talk to me."

I turned around and saw that she was feeling the tips of the tines of her fork. "Uh, it's my *job* to look at you and talk to you," I said.

I went back to my task and turned the stove off, pulling the bottle of milk out of the boiling water. I turned around again to watch the older girl as I blotted the milk on my wrist, and I saw her trying to stick the fork through her hand. Luckily, it was a blunt fork intended for children, so she did no real physical harm.

I decided to handle the situation calmly. This girl, for all her weirdness, was a child and not a demonic force.

I knelt down next to her. She shivered, startled, as if coming out of a trance. "That's not safe. You could really hurt yourself. I know you're curious, but we only use forks for eating."

When the mother got home, I told her quietly what had happened, in the corner by the front door so her daughter wouldn't hear.

"Okay," she said, as I explained. "Okay." And then she invoked the name of the Lord as if a resident of hell was among us. "Jesus!" she yelled, flying to her child, one hand landing on her daughter's forehead, the other in the air. "I call upon you to banish this demon from my daughter! She is your child, my Lord, protect her from the enemy!"

As I watched this mother perform a mini-exorcism on her three-year-old, I could not find a way to rationalize it. By the book, she had not technically done anything wrong. She was within her rights as a Christian mother to protect her child from evil forces. But the child, from my perspective, was not possessed by a demon. She was a weird, creepy little girl who, like many children, was fascinated by the morbid. If I had been allowed, I could have introduced her to the world of Tim Burton movies, and she could have explored her spooky side with stop-motion clay women who sewed their own heads to their bodies. She didn't need an exorcism—she needed an outlet. She needed Halloween, a chance to run amok amid ghouls and eyeball candy.

But she would not get that chance in this world we were in together. She would be told she had a demon in her, and she would need to expel it. In my growing doubt, I could relate to her. I wondered if I, too, would be called dead for being alive.

✷

I wasn't happy, despite my weekly church visits, and I was too tired to read my damn Bible. Worst of all, I was filled with lust, falling for people left and right, with an urge to masturbate that felt like it was taking over my being.

I told myself that what happened with Robert had screwed me up. The truth was that he had been a gateway to a world of dangerous flirtation. I met other men in the writing program who seemed to fall for me at first glance, who pursued me in ways that no Christian had. I was forthright about my beliefs: I was evangelical, I didn't date nonbelievers or have sex or fool around on anyone's couch. Still, we'd become friends, hang out. I'd see New York with them, museums and restaurants and raves. They would admit their feelings, would get drunk and kiss my cheeks, sometimes moving to my forehead—it felt like they were kissing my mind.

I looked forward to those moments as my sole physical outlet. I had feelings, too. I wanted those mind kisses. I'd hold their hands, confuse them. The nice ones would apologize the next morning. "I'm sorry, I shouldn't have done that." I'd accept their apologies, knowing that I had crossed my own boundaries, that I hadn't respected their hearts, their friendship, their time.

They'd move on. Find women who they could have real relationships with. I'd feel broken up with.

And then I met Michael.

He was a fellow writer from The New School. When I'd babysit late into the night, he'd occasionally show up with snacks, and we'd eat, laughing quietly together before my employers came home.

He emailed me one rainy day in the autumn, when the orange leaves were sticking to the buildings: *I've got some Groupons. Wanna get a cheap dinner?*

This became our thing. We'd find the best deals, on burgers, Thai food, crazy pizzas with slices too big to finish. We'd leave satisfied, having dropped only ten dollars on our meal, and continue our conversations during long walks around the city. Michael was dapper—collared shirts under his sweaters, dark hair parted and combed in waves that sat handsomely on his head. He was soft spoken and gentle, emotionally in tune with those around him, a man with friends of all genders who liked sports without machismo. He loved baking, and we'd try out recipes together. Once we baked a sheet of cookies on wax paper, not realizing there was a difference between that and parchment. We couldn't get them off the pan and had to eat the tops off them with forks.

Michael was a spiritual skeptic but not wholly adversarial. He found my faith intriguing and told me he wished he could feel the same way: "I admire the way you think about it all. It gives me hope that maybe there's something out there."

I was determined to pray the Holy Spirit into this man. In my mind, I evolved from being a babysitter to being a parent, living in a Brooklyn brownstone. I imagined Michael walking down our front steps, our child swaddled against his chest as we strode to a quiet brunch spot. Could I have a normal life like that? Could things be so simple, so easy, so smooth? Moments with Michael were like stepping out of a storm, into a warm home with a fire crackling in the hearth. Why did I feel more comfortable with him than I did in my own skin?

Michael's parents lived only a few towns away from Southbridge, and I visited them all once, over Christmas break. When it came time to leave, a severe thunderstorm hit, and Michael invited me to stay over so I didn't have to drive back in bad weather. I agreed apprehensively; I didn't want to put myself in another situation like the one with Robert. But he was so different from Robert, so respectful, so kind. I knew that I was in control of what happened that night. He changed the sheets on his bed and said that he'd take the couch. We stayed up for a few hours, talking about our writing, and when I said it was time for bed, he stood up with me. We hugged, and he held me close, and we didn't let go for several minutes. I wanted to kiss him, but didn't want to ruin our friendship. When I let go, I said goodnight and walked quickly into the bedroom.

I didn't know what to do the next morning, when I smoked my first cigarette on his parents' front stoop as I looked out over a green canal. I didn't know what to do a month later, when we met up for dinner and I did something I was forbidden from doing as a woman in the evangelical world: I told him that my feelings existed, and I wanted to see where they took us. I didn't know what to do when he said he had feelings for me too but didn't know if they were romantic—he needed some time to think about it. I didn't know what to do three months later, when we kissed outside of the subway, and I knew there was no turning back.

I didn't know how to have a relationship with a nonbeliever, but for the first time since converting, I wanted one. A real one.

I knew that a real relationship with Michael wasn't possible unless I got the leaders from my church on board. I was bound to the God of evangelicalism, and the church was his mouthpiece in my life, the arbiter of my decisions. I had been given a simple framework to operate in, and I knew I was testing a dangerous boundary.

"Missionary dating" was the term for it, whispered within the movement like an unofficial swear word. To missionary date was to take a selfish kind of risk, attaching your heart to a zombie in hopes that God would bless your efforts and bring the dead back to life. Its risks were myriad. The relationship could, for example, result in a soul tie but then the person could refuse God's advances, leaving you with no choice but to end the relationship, breaking your own heart and souring your sweetheart's opinion of the faith. Or—an even greater risk—you could end up outside the faith yourself, joining the nonbeliever in their death. What weak human heart could withstand such a test and choose an invisible God over a tangible zombie, when our souls had been designed by God to seek and need physical companionship? Was I strong enough to keep that from happening? Could I have a relationship with Michael at a certain emotional distance?

I contacted Pastor Luke's wife, an amiable woman named Nancy, and explained that I needed to meet and discuss matters of the heart. She understood what this meant—I needed time with a woman alone—and set up a private lunch date at her home. We ate fresh basil salad on her backyard terrace, her plants in bloom, surrounding us like Eden. She sat across from me, her slim arms wrapped in a shawl. I told her about Michael, about our complicated relationship that was verging on romance and his openness to the spiritual realm, and was pleased to sense excitement in her reaction.

"What do you feel God saying?" she asked. This was a question Cate wouldn't have asked. Cate would have just told me what God was saying, or at least implied it.

"I feel like he wants me to take this chance," I told Nancy honestly. "He's saying he wants me to trust him."

Nancy, her cheekbones strong and sturdy as icebergs, reached across the table, enveloping my fingers in the warmth of her hands. "Let's pray," she said. She asked God to bless my interactions with Michael, to keep Satan at bay as the Holy Spirit showed us his way. "We trust you," she prayed. "In your name, amen."

Before I left, buckling my feet into my fraying sandals, she gave only one word of warning—a boundary I couldn't break as I explored what God wanted. "You can't marry Michael," she said, kneeling down to hug me. "You can date him, but you can't marry him if he doesn't come to know Jesus."

And with that, I had my permission.

✵

But after all my precautions, all my efforts, I found myself wholly disappointed in God's follow-through. Four months after deciding that we'd "see where things took us," Michael sat me down on a park bench and told me that he loved me, but only as a friend.

"But . . . how?" I asked. "When did you realize this?"

"Soon after we talked about it. I'm sorry. I feel terrible."

I told him that there was no way it could be true. That kiss outside the subway! How could that be only friendship? He said that he wanted to feel something, that he didn't want to disappoint me, but he couldn't shake the thought that this wasn't right, that it wasn't what he wanted. He told me that he wanted to be my friend forever, and I said that I didn't know how to give him that—to love him in the way I loved him and remain platonic, making emotional room that my heart couldn't handle.

I understood then that I couldn't have a relationship with him at a certain emotional distance, that it couldn't work romantically or platonically, and I had joined him in death without realizing it. I was soul-tied—not even by a relationship but by mere fantasies of brownstones and babies. I was dying because of my daydreams.

✷

My body tried to shut itself down again, throwing up what I put into it. My system went haywire, blood vessels bursting around my eyes. Eating made me nauseous. I got into cabs and imagined accidents, cars ripping toward me as I was cast through the window. These were the consequences, I told myself, of going against God's order. For thinking that a nonbeliever could love me, could give me the type of relationship that my alive-in-God heart was seeking. My Bible had been tucked away for too long. I needed to see a counselor, somebody Christian. I needed to get back on track. I'd strayed so far away I didn't even know where the tracks were. I was too busy losing a third of my body weight and only sleeping three hours a night to search, too busy wishing for a train to hit me so the pain would stop.

How does one die like this over, as Cate said, *just a man*?

But in other parts of myself I knew—this wasn't about a man. It was about something inside me dying that I couldn't look at, couldn't watch as it slipped away. My faith sat bruised by my own curiosity, beaten by my desire. Why couldn't I be alive in God and just enjoy it? Why couldn't I find my satisfaction in him? Like the girl I babysat, I needed something that I wasn't allowed to have, because needing it was on the verge of demonic. Would I, too, need to exorcise myself?

17.

I am, if nothing else, a person who makes one hell of an effort. When I was twelve, in an attempt to climb the social ranks of my middle school, I spent the fifty dollars my grandparents sent me for Christmas on holiday presents for the popular girls, even though I promised my father I wouldn't. The girls were confused because, (A) We weren't friends, and (B) it was only December 1st. "Um, thanks?" one said, looking at her new Seafoam Dreams body spray. "But are you trying to say that we smell?"

But when Kayla Sheldon's mother drove her to my house so she could gift me a candle and a ceramic flower, I learned that my sowing could result in reaping. If I put in enough effort, a popular girl might materialize on my doorstep. All I had to do was give it my all, lie to my father, and spend fifty dollars.

So I don't want you to think that I didn't try to fix my faith disease. But the harder I tried, the worse it got. Whether it was from swearing or kissing or having crushes on nonbelievers or some demon entering my soul, something had snapped inside of me, a very vital tendon. I began to find sermons annoying, my favorite pastors trite, the Bible itself vapid.

"Ananias and Sapphira died because they could not surrender their lives to the Lord," a guest pastor preached one Sunday. He was retelling a story from Acts 5:1–11 about a married couple who sold a piece of property to help start the early church but lied to the apostles about the full sum they received, giving only a portion and keeping the rest for themselves. Catching them in their lie, God struck them both dead, and the pastor blamed it on their inability to fully trust God, to give everything about themselves completely to him.

Were those two deaths really necessary? I wondered. Wasn't it understandable that they were ambivalent about giving all their money to some random guys who rolled into town? This didn't line up with the God I thought I had given my life to, a God of compassion who let Thomas feel the holes in his side when he doubted, a God who made room for questions and fear, who soothed the minds of his children when they made mistakes, who endured a brutal death to pay for their sins and reunite with them again. Who was this other God, this penny-pincher who demanded total submission? This dictator who killed those he claimed to love? A being who couldn't get out of his own way, stumbling around his majestic clouds, exerting power through deadly, imperialistic force?

Why hadn't he struck me dead, too? Like Ananias and Sapphira, I was keeping plenty of things to myself, plenty of secrets from the followers of Christ around me. For example: Michael. Despite what he'd said that night on the park bench, I was not convinced he didn't love me romantically, and I put all my effort into convincing him of this fact, even though I knew it was the worst kind of missionary dating. I'd wear my best pairs of skinny jeans when I saw him, hair tossed back voluptuously in pins, trying hard to look like I wasn't really trying. "I can't be friends with you," I'd say, red lipstick staining the edge of my wineglass, "because we're not friends. We're in love."

"But we are friends, aren't we?" he'd say. "Are you sure that I have feelings for you?"

I'd feel vindicated. How could someone who *didn't* have

feelings say that? I would take him back to the beginning—the Groupon dates, the long walks—and point out everything he'd done that suggested feelings stronger than friendship. I'd insist there was something he hadn't worked through, some roadblock in his mind that kept him from discovering the depths of his love. "Is it the fact that I'm a Christian?" I asked. "Are you confused because of my faith?"

"No!" he said. "It has nothing to do with that."

And then one day, he sent an email back that broke the cycle: *When I tell you how I feel, you tell me that I feel another way. And I feel like you're not respecting my words, and in that way, you're crossing boundaries.*

I was aghast. In my mind, *I* was the victim in all of this—not him! How dare he accuse me of such behavior! All I was doing was pointing out things he had said and done, and then questioning the explanations he gave until he felt like his explanations were wrong!

I was humiliated. I wrote Michael an email back telling him to never reach out to me again.

As this was unfolding, there was another thing I kept hidden from everyone: I continued to vomit whatever entered my body. My weight dropped drastically, my desire for satiation secondary to the ways I wanted to govern it. The relief of vomiting! The release of pressure, nausea no longer swelling within me. *You've let it go*, I heard. *You're not carrying it anymore.* What had I let go? All of my food, but also grief and anxiety. I wanted to get rid of the pain. This, at least, was in my control. God was controlling my life, but I was controlling this.

This was where my efforts had landed me. Heartbreak, vomit, chaos. My mind brimming with confusion and questions. What did I have to offer the friends I was trying to convert? I was the empty one. I couldn't even keep a sandwich down.

No, no—I was full, full in God! My friends were the ones who were sinners! Right? I knew the logic, the apologetics. I knew what I was supposed to believe. I just wasn't sure I believed it.

*

Will was struggling too. By 2012, a year after graduation, he had moved into a three-bedroom apartment with our poet friend Erin and another woman he knew from online. The plan was to build upon our ministry, to create a natural meeting ground that would help our spiritual conversations turn seamlessly into Bible studies. But it appeared to be backfiring. Will took to locking himself in his room and listening to music all day. Our regular in-person hangouts turned into text conversations in which he would complain about the state of sexual sin in his living environment. "It's really hard being around this all the time," he typed. "Both my roommates are bringing guys home. I can hear them going at it."

"We set up shop in a hellhole," I reminded him. "We don't get to be comfortable here. This is the price we pay for showing Jesus to lost people."

As I went out into the land of zombies, trying to inject their minds with spiritual serum, Will dug further into our church, setting new roots down there, spending all his time with fellow believers in Christ. He was no longer putting effort into our ministry.

You worship the writers, he texted me one day.

The writers are fun, I responded, like a rebellious child. Was Cate right about me? Was I still in the midst of a spiritual adolescence?

I know, Will said, *but they're only good for us in doses.*

Will and I were supposed to protect each other. We had promised to be truthful to each other, to be the voices of God in one another's lives as we waded through the difficulties of our ministry. We were partners in many ways, bound together by friendship in the Holy Spirit, but now, the bond between us was tearing. We argued often. He told me that I shouldn't have tried to start a romantic relationship with a nonbeliever like Michael in the first place and therefore had no right to be angry about what happened. I told him he was shutting himself off from me and our friends, that he had left me on this spiritual battlefield alone, trying to shoot enough arrows for both of us. He told me that I was turning into the people I was trying to convert, and that if I so much as smoked a cigarette with them, he would stop going to my church and find another community of believers.

Little did he know that I smoked cigarettes with them all the time. I had even learned how to pack a bowl with marijuana buds.

When Pastor Luke asked what I thought of making Will our church's worship leader, I told him it was a horrible idea. "He's not spiritually mature enough for that. He doesn't even read the Bible." I claimed to speak the truth in love: he wasn't at church for God, he was there for the comforts of community.

Pastor Luke made him the worship leader anyway, and I felt obstinate, angry. I told myself I wanted more for Will than that, but I wasn't sure what that meant.

✷

I visited Cate in New Jersey. We had chicken and veggies for dinner, homemade ice cream for dessert. In the morning, over cups of coffee, I told her what had happened with Michael. I hadn't shared it with her before. We hadn't talked much over the past year, plus I hadn't really wanted her opinion—I was hearing enough of Will's.

"Well, now I know why you've been so quiet," she said. "You know this was inappropriate, right? You know what I would have said."

I told her that I'd talked to my pastor's wife about it. I was in communication with church leadership. I wasn't hiding my love for this person from my community.

"Oh, really? And what did your pastor's wife say?"

"She said that I couldn't marry him if he didn't become a believer. But I had hope that he'd come around."

"Missionary dating is a bad idea, always. I've told you that before. And look how this turned out." She was referring to the near-bulimic episodes I was having, the turmoil in my mind and body. "You went where you weren't supposed to go."

I went home angry. She hadn't been through it all. She didn't know what it had been like. She was maps, logic, and boxes. Her emotions were not triggered unless those factors fell into place. Mine seemed to be triggered all the time.

✷

I met Becca in the summer of 2012 through one of my writer friends. Eleanor and I, now living in Brooklyn, were looking for a roommate, and he thought she would be a good fit. "She has the same belief system as you," my friend said. "I think you'd really like each other."

When we talked on the phone, she seemed normal, nice, laid-back. She was looking to move to the city from the Midwest. The church she attended was large, made up mainly of college students and those who ministered to them. This, I could tell, was a real Christian woman. Someone who led Bible studies, discipled people, put on after-church potluck dinners in her home. Making her our third roommate was an effort to rekindle my zeal. I thought living with her might be like what I experienced living with believers on Summer Project.

Becca packed her belongings in a moving truck and drove all the way to the East Coast. She brought side tables and ball jars, frilly lamps and carpets with her, the kind of décor that Eleanor and I had long been without. Within the first two weeks, she was making peach and basil pizza for us, her pans too large to fit in our half-size stove. She had to cut the dough in quarters and put it on cookie sheets, serving slices to Eleanor and me over the course of two hours. It was sweet and surprising, a new combination, heaps of mozzarella melted over fruit.

The three of us, as roommates, formed a new combination. Eleanor was shy, quiet, and introverted, while I was a moderate-tempered ambivert. Becca, in contrast, was loud in her opinions and her actions, her footsteps heavy in our home. Her laugh was an explosion, her wardrobe colors vibrant, her very presence unmistakable. She and I spent entire weekends together, cooking dinner, watching movies, riding bikes. We'd roll fast down hills, Becca whooping behind me. Moments were to her a celebration of the fact we were alive. She was fresh air for me in a time that felt so stale.

We went to churches, service hopping on Sundays. Mine in the morning, sometimes hers, another at night if we could cram it all in. On the train we shared stories of our faith, how we got to where we were. She was born to young parents—children themselves, she said, who didn't have the full mental and emotional capacity to raise her. Thank God they took her to church, where she met Christian women who acted as surrogate mothers and molded her into the person she had become.

I told her about coming to know Christ through Cru, how I was in a weird funk but was trying to figure it out. I'd decided to see a Christian psychiatrist from the counseling center in Tim Keller's church, and I was waiting for my first appointment. Maybe I needed medication to help me stop throwing everything up. Maybe it would help me see again, figure out what was really wrong.

"It sounds like Campus Crusade really screwed you up," Becca said. Though she said she hadn't personally gone through anything like that, she diagnosed the problem. It was not the belief system itself; it was the way I was raised in it, the influence of Cate and the organization. "I have some resources that can help you," she said, retrieving a packet of papers from her room. "This will explain a lot."

I took the papers to my room, eager for some relief from my intangible doubt. I opened the packet, read a couple pages. It was about Calvinism. The ins and outs of the theology. I knew this already. How was it supposed to help me?

Then the realization came tumbling into view: Becca, in a spiritual sense, was the person I had been three years prior, someone who thought that the right theology could solve all problems. Emotional anguish got you down? You're just not thinking about things right. Can't stop daydreaming about death? Here, read this PDF on limited atonement. The hard work of feeling was absent, and I saw that so clearly in Becca. She was who Cate had trained me to be, and I was slowly becoming her foil.

✷

Cate called onc day, wanting to catch up. The last time we talked had been when I visited her, nine months earlier. We were both busy with our separate lives, she a married woman with a classroom to run, I a young single person getting back on my mental feet. I had recently stopped throwing up meals and was sleeping six hours a night instead of three. The Prozac my Christian psychiatrist prescribed finally seemed to be working, the clouds in my brain beginning to part. I was even trying my hand at a copywriting internship, though the advertising industry was the last place I expected a young Christian woman to be.

But the questions about my faith remained. That core evangelical doctrine that said salvation only came through accepting Jesus Christ as your Lord and Savior—it had been bothering me again.

"Joseph and I have some questions about salvation, too," Cate said, to my surprise. "We've wondered if there are different ways that God sees people believing in Jesus, even if it's not the way we traditionally think of belief."

I couldn't believe my luck. Finally, someone from the Christian world was getting what I was saying! And Cate of all people—my teacher of teachers!

"Totally," I said. "And also, the whole idea of sex before marriage being a sin. I've been thinking a lot about that. Is it really? Like, could it—"

Cate cut me off. "No, no. That's not up for debate."

"What? Sex?"

"How could you honestly think that? Sex before marriage is absolutely a sin. God would never condone that. The Bible is clear. I don't see how you could make an argument against it."

I was silent. Here Cate was, entertaining the idea that the whole foundation of our belief system might be flawed, but the idea of sex before marriage was absolutely unconscionable to her.

As we hung up, I realized I had found Cate's limits, where her logic ended and her emotions began.

✷

After that, my questions exploded. Who wrote the books of the Old Testament, anyway? For how long were the stories told through oral tradition before someone finally wrote them down? Who was on the council that put the Bible together, and how did they decide which books made it in and which didn't? Who gave them the authority? How do we know it was God? What if the apostle Paul was just writing letters that were never supposed to be stamped holy scripture? Who decided that we needed to live our lives according to his ramblings to the Ephesians, and why? I needed to know how I could trust the past six years of my life. If these foundational questions couldn't be answered, if Paul's letters weren't infallible, then what was I doing? What was I depriving myself for? Why was I living in terror that the majority of the world was going to hell and working every moment of my life to save them?

I asked Pastor Luke these questions after church one day in the spring of 2013, as we packed sandwiches in large coolers for a picnic.

"I have resources for you," he said. "I'm going to send them."

I emailed him a reminder later that week. I was desperate, in crisis. I needed to know where this all came from to keep going.

No email with resources came from Pastor Luke. Instead, the next Sunday, he referenced my questions at the pulpit. "The formation of the Bible? The reasons this piece was chosen and not that? I don't need to know that, I don't need to dig into those holes to have faith that God was in charge."

My eyes welled like a shore at high tide. If I couldn't get answers, I at least wanted to hear that my questions were valid and understandable. But instead, my spiritual father figure, without a glance in my direction, announced that they didn't matter to him in front of our whole family. Surely as someone who spent so much time thinking about the word of God, he had asked similar questions at some point. Didn't he have any answers? Or had these questions threatened him in the same way they were threatening me?

✷

Perhaps, I thought, I needed to focus my efforts on spending more time with Christian women. Christian men did not feel safe to me. Their presence often clouded women's judgment, our words, our thoughts. They had privileges that we didn't. They got to ask us out, lead our churches, be the heads of households. I wanted to know how *women* felt and what that meant for this God I wanted to keep. I wanted to search the depths of this faith with them, crawl through the tunnels, see what we found. How long would we be under, and where would we surface? Did anyone else wonder if we were wasting our time?

I started attending a weekly Bible study at Becca's church, which was in Brooklyn, closer to our apartment. It was led by a woman named Haley. Her voice was deep but serene, her perspective thoughtful. As we read the Bible, she managed to question without complaining, lamenting the difficulties of God's truth, getting us to pray together for his glory. She asked him to show us his goodness through our sadness.

It was exactly what I wanted. A group that acknowledged how messed up this all felt, that didn't turn away from what we couldn't understand and call God good when he felt like the opposite. A gathering of women that asked hard questions, that implored God to show us his heart, to help us see where it was going. Week by week, we opened up about our struggles—with faith, with sexuality, with the very things that made us human. I told them about my questions and how they felt unanswerable, and we prayed that God would soothe me enough to show me his truth in time. While I had gone off Prozac in an effort to let God handle my mental issues himself, I learned that over half the group was on antidepressants. I was, however, the only one who hadn't partaken in sex. These women were experienced in ways that I wasn't, but they had all come to the same conclusion: they were broken and needed Jesus.

One night, a woman told us about a man she had been sleeping with. He was a nonbeliever and occasionally used cocaine, but she wasn't sure if she wanted to end their relationship. Haley, with fervent compassion, said the relationship needed to cease, no matter how difficult that was. The woman nodded—she seemed to be expecting as much—and tears started to fall from her eyes.

Haley put a hand on her back, beckoning us all to stand and do the same. "Father God," she said, "I pray that you release our sister in Christ from the temptation of sexual sin, that you fill those parts of her heart with your lasting satisfaction. By miracle, halt the contact this man has with her, make it easier for her to let go than she realizes. Give her the strength to live like you would, to wait for the beautiful future you've set aside for her."

The woman's skin felt cool, almost damp beneath my fingertips. Was she beginning to sweat? Did she really want this? I wanted to wipe my hand on my jeans. I wanted to give this woman the space to make her own decision, to stop crowding her, telling her what she was supposed to choose. But she welcomed our choice. She asked us to make it for her. Evangelicalism taught her that it didn't matter what she wanted because she couldn't trust her own desires.

I couldn't stop myself from wondering what gave *us* the ability to do that for her. If we couldn't do it for ourselves, how could we do it for someone else?

⁕

I wasn't done trying. I traveled to the mountains of Colorado for a Christian women's retreat, where I lay belly-down in a small room with six women pulling my legs and six other women pulling the exercise band I was clutching as I tried to move forward with only my elbows.

"I'm not ugly!" I yelled into the carpet. "God made me beautiful!"

"You're gross, you're terrible, no one would ever want you," the women with my legs snarled.

"I love you!" the women with the elastic band shouted. "You are loved!"

This was supposed to be a way for my brain to work through its greatest struggles and connect with God. We had all been asked to write down our most difficult emotional issues, and I wrote that mine was feeling beautiful, wondering if maybe the root of my spiritual crisis was a fear that I was not worthy of love after all my rejection from men.

We had done a similar exercise for a woman who felt useless, another for a woman who dealt with anger. For a woman who was afraid her son had committed suicide because of her, we ran in a circle around her as she cried, "God? God?" until she burst through us and wrapped up the woman playing God in an embrace. Asked by the leaders how they felt after their exercises, all the women answered positively: "Released." "Healed." "Found."

How I wanted to feel that way, too. Instead, I felt like I was being hypnotized in a high school assembly; I couldn't let go enough to convince myself that the voice of God was coming from the women in front of me. So I put up a fake tussle, fake broke free, and group hugged the women by my head. I lied and said I felt peaceful. Why ruin it for the others?

On my last night there, we did an activity in which we all lay down on the floor and closed our eyes. "Imagine a box in front of you," the speaker said. "There's a lock on the front. What do you want to put in it?"

The answers came easily. *My mom*, I thought. *My sister Emily. My sister Gillian. My dad. My brother Matt.* Was there room still? *Erin. Jack. Morgan. Ben. Michael.* The entirety of New York. My hope for them all.

And in that box, I put a version of all those people, the Christians I wanted them to be, the Christians I wasn't sure they would ever be. I put away my desire to make them real, to live in the light of God with them, to bring them into this godly cage with me. I let them sit, stand, rest. I made them small so they could all fit comfortably in their own spaces.

✷

The theologian G. K. Chesterton wrote, "The more I considered Christianity, the more I found that while it had established a rule and order, the chief aim of that order was to give room for good things to run wild."

I found the opposite to be true. The more I considered Christianity, the fewer good things I saw. The chief aim of it all seemed to be to build an army, gain control. I did not want to fight for that cause anymore. I did not want to pass something on to others that was making me want to die.

It was at this point, after a world of effort to save it, that my faith found its end.

I made the official decision to stop believing in late 2013, in a moment I wasn't expecting. I had spent four days by myself, and I was watching the first season of *American Horror Story* while sewing buttons on a coat. There was something about the gore and the ghosts, combined with the concentration on slow, meticulous work, that pushed me over an edge, and I wandered into parts of myself I hadn't spoken to in seven years. It was the space between learning and knowing, the moment before you make a choice. It was a communion with the person I used to be, who had been left on another side of myself, the person who had asked Cate, in an attempt to grow closer to her, "Why do you think God sends people to hell?"

In a way, I was still waiting for an answer, seven years later, after the tract booklets and mission trips, after the Bible studies and prayer sessions, after the worship bands and weekend retreats. Cate thought God sent people to hell because the price of sin was death, but that no longer seemed like a strong enough reason when there was so much good around me, when I found the *imago dei* in sinners who were better people than the God I worshiped.

Who was that person? I missed her. Even though she was broken, I missed her. It was time to bring her back.

18.

It was New Year's Eve, 2013, the same week I sewed the buttons on my coat, the same week I reacquainted myself with the person I was sitting on my dorm-room bed, facing Cate, asking her about God. If there was a God, he wasn't who I'd thought he was the past seven years, and in light of that, I needed to figure out who I was. I was shaky in my reclaimed identity, unsure as I stepped into the world that night, hair pinned into a style that looked like it was from the 1920s. I walked out in my coat, knowing that I had the freedom to kiss someone, to be a person I wasn't sure how to be.

I took the subway by myself and went to the new apartment of my old downstairs neighbors, a bottle of prosecco in hand. I ran into Nick. Oh yeah, that guy! I'd met him at another party several months earlier. Awkward dude, with wiry old-man glasses and a weird sort of charm. We started talking, and didn't stop for an hour. He got me another drink and I touched his arm, feeling a spiritual tendon snap.

I knew I'd sent a signal.

Around one in the morning, when I got up to leave, Nick asked me to stay.

"Nah, I'm tired," I said.

"Do you want to get a drink? Right now?"

"Okay."

We walked down a snowy street and found a bar, and I sat at a table as he bought us drinks. When we left, he hooked his fingers in mine and didn't let go as we made our way to the subway. I felt a warmth in parts of my body that, previously, I wasn't supposed to acknowledge. As we waited for the train, he held me from behind. He kissed the back of my head, then my cheek, and then I turned around and grabbed his face and kissed him like I wanted to.

✷

I slept with Nick twice over the course of two dates. The first time, my body moved out of instinct and lust, but I didn't know how to open up, how to make room for him. He took control of the situation and forced his fingers inside me—moving hard, fast, harder—until I stung and bled. I didn't know any other way to make it happen, so I let him. He was more experienced than I was. I accepted the pain as a part of "virginity's" loss—a rite of passage into a world I was late entering.

By the second date, we managed to have some semblance of intercourse.

A day later, I was burning, which I thought must be normal.

Two days after that, I sat embarrassed in the emergency clinic as the doctor explained how sick I could have gotten. Another day and the urinary tract infection could have spread to my kidneys and caused serious complications. "You have to pee after sex," he told me. "Go to the bathroom no more than two minutes after."

He seemed to regard this as common knowledge. I wondered if everyone else in the adult world knew about this except me.

✷

"So you're just not Christian anymore. All of that was for nothing. It's gone now? Just like that?" Emily erupted over the phone, magma seeping through the speakers, singeing my ears as I tried to talk her down.

"I'm doing things differently now," I said.

"After everything you said?"

"I know, I'm sorry."

"No, you don't understand. I was fourteen, and you told me that sex before marriage would ruin my life. You scared the hell out of me. And now you're calling me to ask questions about sex like none of that ever happened?"

How do you maintain your dignity when you've come popping out of fundamentalism after a tumultuous seven years in which you've told your loved ones they're going to hell unless they agree with you? *Just kidding! I'm not in a cult anymore!*

"You don't get to just flip a switch," Emily said. "You can't just call me and act like you never believed what you did."

Emily wanted atonement, and I didn't know how to give that to her. I also didn't know how to explain that I was suffering in my own way—I was twenty-six and didn't know how to avoid a UTI, or if Nick was right when he said that fingering me for ten minutes would "loosen me up."

I needed my sister, but my sister was hurting. In her view, I couldn't just waltz back into her world of belief as if I hadn't been antagonizing it for nearly a decade.

Somewhere during that time, her cystic fibrosis had stabilized. There was no more need for nebulizers, the shaking vests, the daily doses of steroids that would obliterate infections. She didn't believe in Jesus, but part of my prayers had been answered. Was Jesus to thank? Was he giving me time to help him convert her? Was he staving off her illness so we could have more time to save her soul? Or was the truth that she had never needed to be "saved"?

I submitted myself to her pain as she told me how my beliefs had scarred her young mind. Her childhood was spent in fear she would go to hell, a voice in the back of her brain saying that fire would engulf her unless she gave in. When she started having sex, she felt my judgment from afar, my worldview climbing in to tell her that what she was doing was wrong.

How was it fair, she asked, that I shouldn't feel the same judgment?

"I am," I told her. "I am."

*

I wasn't sure who to turn to when it came to technical questions about sex. My sister was too angry, and I was too embarrassed to ask most of my writing friends. Out of desperation, I went to see Ruth.

Ruth had been a member of the all-women's Bible study I was a part of in Brooklyn, the one where we laid hands on the woman who couldn't stop sleeping with a nonbeliever and prayed for God to make it easy for her to let go. When I first met Ruth, she complimented me on my sense of humor, saying, "I love it when a woman isn't afraid to be funny." She was interesting and smart, and loved theater and stories and talking smack about the patriarchy, openly questioning the sexism she felt the church displayed toward women. When a male member of the church once remarked he would find it unattractive if a woman asked him out, she snapped, "What's so wrong with a woman wanting something?"

Moments like this made me wonder if Ruth might accept me in my new state of post-belief.

I entered her apartment after a brisk bike ride, and she greeted me with a light hug; she was not the type to show much affection. We sat on her couch together sipping cups of warm chamomile tea, and I told her about my experience at the emergency clinic. She didn't seem surprised or appalled that my "virginity" was gone. She didn't cry like Cate would have. She told me that drinking cranberry juice would help me avoid UTIs, and that the doctor was right, always pee after sex, or after any fingering, licking, or other action down there. I felt safe in a warm bath of useful information. I had so many questions, and here Ruth was, open to all of them. Was this what it was like to have a big sister? One who understood the archaic family we came from, who would pass down her knowledge to protect me from pain?

She told me about her experience in graduate school, with a man she was still friends with. They didn't have intercourse, but they did everything else, and she had learned all about sexual health through that. It was important, she said, for women to know how to take care of themselves after sex. It wasn't right to have that information withheld because of an expectation that we'd live our lives perfectly and only experience those things after marriage. Her candidness inspired me, broke a dam of curiosity that flooded my mind. I had walked into that apartment embarrassed by my lack of knowledge, but talking about sex, I discovered, could be fun.

✷

I had sex with Nick again, and again, and again. We rarely planned it; I'd just get a text from him on a Saturday night, casual, asking what I was up to. Then he'd show up at my doorstep, sometimes sober, frequently not, and I'd sneak him into my room, hiding his presence from Becca. She didn't like him or what we were doing in my corner of the apartment, and I was beginning to resent her self-righteousness.

After we had sex, the space between my legs would be on fire, accompanied by a constant feeling that I had to pee. I'd go to the emergency clinic, tell them my symptoms. They'd send me away with a preemptive prescription, telling me that the test results would be back in two days. Each time, I'd start taking the medication, and each time I'd get a phone call: "UTI is negative. You're healthy. Have a good day!"

So why was I burning down there all the time?

I made an appointment with a primary care doctor and then a gynecologist. They conducted tests, told me I was fine, that my vulva and urinary tract looked completely normal. "They don't feel normal," I said. "I'm in pain." Eventually they suggested that I see a urologist, who performed a sonogram and then referred me to a radiologist who scanned the lower half of my body. I was grateful for the thorough attention and care these doctors gave to my concerns, but when the scan results came in, they said once again that my body was completely normal. Nothing was wrong.

Out of ideas, the urologist opened his desk and pulled out a package of samples. "I give these to my patients with overactive bladders. Let's see if these work, and I'll give you a prescription." Judging by the ages of everyone else in the waiting room, this medicine was intended for people fifty years older than me.

I went home, put the pills on my desk, and lay down in bed, where I saw a text from my friend Julie.

Besides Will, Julie was my only friend from The New School who knew Jesus. She had actually been raised evangelical but had left the faith—until she emailed me one semester asking to get a drink because "something crazy just happened." At a bar around the corner from her apartment, she told me, "I prayed for the first time in ten years last night, and afterward, I levitated." The morning after that, God had spoken directly into her mind, asking her to walk to the cemetery so he could show her that he was real. He surprised her with a swarm of butterflies at the entrance.

I was thrilled for her, and also for myself. There was nothing more exciting than hearing a word from God via somebody who could *actually* hear him—it made me feel like I wasn't crazy for holding on to these beliefs. It seemed that God had bestowed a prophetic gift upon Julie, and now I had a friend who saw cool stuff in the spiritual realm. She was fresh-faced every time we met at the bar, as if she had just come home from a honeymoon with God and I was there to receive the souvenir she'd brought back for me. I'd tell her about my troubles, and she'd tell me what God whispered in her ear.

One time, she reached across the table, grabbed my wrist, held it tight. "He wants me to tell you that you're going to love the man he has for you."

"Really?" I said, tears welling. "He has someone for me?"

"Oh yes, yes. And he's better than you can imagine."

Things then took a strange turn when Julie began showing up to the bar tired, darkness under her eyes, her spine straight and alert as if someone had followed her there. "God hasn't been good to me lately," she told me. She'd seen an evil presence at her office, a man with an overlay of bleeding arteries on his face, as if a scythe had torn off layers of his skin. In addition, when homeless people walked past her on the train, she could hear the demons in their heads. We prayed that God would protect her from those kinds of frightening images, but it kept happening. I wanted to believe that God could help her, that a pipe had burst in the spiritual realm and he could repair it. But deeper, in that small piece of pre-conversion me that still existed, I wondered, *Is this really God? Or is this mental illness?*

Now, years later, as I weighed the pros and cons of bladder meds, Julie texted me: *Want to grab a drink?*

We went to a bar and I cried and told her about the doctor's appointments, about the UTI that wouldn't go away. I told her that I was having sex but my body wasn't taking to it, that it felt wrong, that I was scared I wasn't made like normal people.

"Maybe it's in your head," Julie said.

"What do you mean?" I asked, surprised her reaction wasn't more, well, Christian.

"I mean, maybe you're freaking yourself out. Maybe you're afraid that God is angry at you, and this is how it's coming out."

Of course. The idea that had started it all: Sex before marriage is a sin that will result in soul ties, a broken spirit, something that can't be healed without God. It was dignifying in the evangelical world to save sex for marriage, to uphold a sense of propriety by abstaining until holy matrimony. In my new life, it was dignifying to have sex when I wanted to, to let my body experience something it desired. But it was not easy to let go of the idea, to change my definition of dignity. When a glass has been broken on the floor, you have to be careful to make sure the smallest shards have been swept away. You cannot always see what's been left behind when something shatters—and the smallest pieces can be the least visible, and the most dangerous.

I checked in with myself, with the parts that had been burning. They were cool and calm. The pain had disappeared.

✷

Eight months after leaving my faith, I began to receive strange phone calls. The first came while I was at work. A man's voice. "You've got a secret admirer," he hissed. "Someone loves you and you don't even know it. He loves the way you walk and talk."

"Who is this?"

"It's me. You're just so pretty."

I hung up, disturbed. This had to be a prank.

I received another call about a week later. I was in bed, a book on my lap. This time, the voice was a woman. "I know what you did," she seethed, consonants snapping. "I saw you. I know what you did."

I hung up much quicker this time, and put my phone face down on the bedside table.

The third and final call came while I was visiting my family in Massachusetts. We were eating lunch. A young woman's voice. "I'm calling to see how you're feeling."

"Fine. Who is this?"

"You were in the hospital last night."

"Um, no I wasn't."

"Yes, you were," she said. "You were unconscious."

"I was on a bus . . . "

"You were unconscious! Oh my God, you need to come back right now!"

I hung up again.

When I got back to New York, I contacted Julie to get her perspective on the situation. Although I had left the church, I was still unsure about the kinds of things she saw, not fully convinced she wasn't tapping into some kind of spiritual realm. Did I want to believe it because it could benefit me? Was I unready to let go of the comfort of having a prophetic friend? Was it too hard to leave the God of evangelicalism behind entirely—not just the dogma, but the mystery, the idea of a world beyond my understanding?

"Demons," Julie said. "No doubt at all, God just told me. You've done something to open yourself up to them. We need to pray now."

I was against the idea at first. After all I had been through, all that had changed about me, all the beliefs I had cracked open and exposed as sexism or homophobia, how could I return and ask the evangelical God who had abused me for help? What use was there in praying again, in groveling at the feet of a tyrant? I went along with it because it felt awkward not to, and I tried to believe that the phone calls would stop.

And they did stop. My phone remained free of strange numbers, no more voices haunting me.

Then I got together with my high school friend Ben, right after Christmas. We were at a fusion restaurant, eating teriyaki chicken, small umbrellas bobbing in our fluorescent tiki drinks.

"I was getting these weird phone calls," I told him.

He started coughing, spit some of his drink out onto the table.

"Are you okay?" I asked.

"The one about you being in the hospital? That one was my favorite."

As it turned out, Ben had given my number to some stupid prank-call radio show. There were no demons involved. Julie was wrong.

I realized that dignity was not just about me. It was about looking at situations as they were, honoring someone enough not to view mental illness as a spiritual experience in the hopes of reinforcing your own belief system. It brought me back to college, when Brianna from Campus Crusade had paced the church parking lot talking to herself, and Cate and I tried to bolster our faith with her suffering, to see it as proof that spiritual attack was real. I no longer wanted to believe something at the expense of another person. I didn't want to comfort myself with someone else's pain.

19.

From the start, Nick had a knife-like edge that he pointed at me when I least expected it. I felt it for the first time on our second date, when we were standing in the subway station, heading back to my apartment. We were kissing, drunk on beer, when my nose brushed against his. He jerked back like a hornet had flown at his face.

"Fuck! Are you stupid?"

I stepped back, brought my hands up slowly. I tried to make eye contact, but he wasn't looking. "I wasn't trying to hurt you."

"I know. I just have a sensitive nose."

I put my hands in my pockets, turned my body to the tracks.

When we got on the train, he apologized.

"I'm sorry," he said. "I got in a bar fight last week. Haven't fully healed."

A bar fight? Was this what secular people did? Still, I forgave him. Kissed him. At least he acknowledged what he did, and took action to make me feel better.

A few months later, at the end of the summer, we went to dinner for his birthday. I made sure he got his dessert with no singing, exactly like I knew he wanted. I held my phone up to take a picture of him sheepishly smiling behind a chocolate cake and a candle.

The smile was gone by the time I took the picture. "What are you gonna do with that?" he said.

"The picture?"

"Yeah."

"I don't know. Put it on Facebook?"

"No Facebook," he said. "Especially no tags."

"Why?" I asked. I wondered if he was secretly married. Was I a mistress, unbeknownst to myself?

"I don't need people knowing my business," he said.

On the train back to my place, he shared his opinion on wage disparity between men and women. "Why would I argue against something I benefit from?" he said.

"Because empathy. Compassion. You're talking to a woman who works, too."

"That's not my problem. It's yours."

I went silent, got off the train without looking at him, walked up the subway steps as he followed behind. What was wrong with this person I had fallen for, who was already such an intimate part of my life, who paid the two-hundred-dollar restaurant bill when I was in the bathroom? What would the church have said about Nick in that moment? That he was manning up. Fulfilling his role. I couldn't tell the difference between their approval and mine. I wanted to feel the depths of a real relationship. I wanted him to apologize, to explain the undercurrent of his words—why they felt so sinister.

"You take things so seriously," he said when we got back to my apartment. "You really need to lighten up."

So he was kidding. At that moment, it was easier for me to let it go than make him take responsibility.

He liked to joke about cheating on me, pointing out girls on TV, on the sidewalk. *He's just joking*, I'd tell myself, trying to learn from his past responses that he didn't mean anything by it.

I tried once to joke back. "Oh yeah, she's hot," I said of the girl he was talking about. "Let's have a threesome, that would be fun!"

"You're lying," he said. "Shut up."

These were his jokes. I wasn't allowed to join.

I held on to the early moments of our relationship, those very first nights. Walking out of the crowded bar before we kissed for the first time, his fingers meeting mine. Our third date, when he took my arm in the middle of the street, pulled me into himself, hugged me, kissed my forehead and my lips. The second month, when I asked him how much he liked me, and he cupped my face in his hands and said, "More than the sun and the moon and the stars."

Those moments grew rarer the longer we dated. By the sixth month, I reached for his hand on the sidewalk, and he moved it toward his chest.

"I don't like holding hands," he said. "It makes me look weak."

I talked often about my past in evangelicalism—I had only just begun to process it. I was filled with knowledge and trauma, exploding with information, piecing anecdotes together into a tapestry of spiritual abuse. I stood back to examine, pulled him in to look, asked him if he saw what I was seeing.

"Only stupid people get involved in stuff like that," he said. "Anyone who falls for that shit is an idiot."

✷

I was, of course, aware of the stereotypes about evangelicals as credulous fools, but it was so different from what I'd experienced at churches that ate Reformation-era theology for breakfast and washed it down with Augustine and Calvin. I was perhaps never more aware of them than when—still deep in the bowels of evangelicalism, rejected by Michael, unable to eat or sleep—I tried speaking in tongues at the behest of my Christian counselor. She said it was easier than people realized and "actually quite innate." Tongues, according to her, were God-inspired sounds, a language that the Holy Spirit spoke, unknown to humans. They would be spoken through my mouth if the Holy Spirit filled me, and God would use them to communicate to my soul. Pray to God for the gift of tongues, and he would bestow it upon you.

This wasn't any more out there than other things I'd heard in the church, like *Satan will give you depression if you live with a Buddha statue* or *You really shouldn't divorce someone, even if they hit you.* I was desperate for some relief. I needed something to work when everything else about my faith was failing, needed to hear from him if I wasn't going to crumple to the ground.

So I sat at the foot of my bed and prayed out loud. "God, I want to experience your healing. Please, give me the gift of tongues."

I waited a minute, unsure of how this would go, not wanting to be disappointed if he didn't give me this gift.

My mouth opened. "Aya shan salah bru hayam salash," I said. Over and over, that gibberish phrase. I rested into it, closed my eyes, tried to see the way I would if I were falling asleep into a lucid dream. I saw a leaf surrounded in light, cupped like the palm of a hand, floating in my vision with a drop of something inside of it. I tried harder. The drop formed into an outline of a person, hairless, a stick figure, resting on its side.

I stopped speaking, opened my eyes, got my journal. *You're telling me that you're holding me through this,* I wrote. *You're telling me to relax. Is that what you're saying?*

My Christian counselor said that I had definitely had an authentic spiritual experience. "That's what tongues are like," she said. "They don't feel like some big revelation. They're just you showing up and letting the Holy Spirit speak through you. It's not like seeing a ghost."

I remembered my mother's ghost story, how natural she said it was. Her brother walking into her classroom, completely translucent. Sitting on the teacher's desk, mouthing words she couldn't hear but somehow understood. He told her that he was okay. According to evangelicalism, my mother saw a demon, but the way she described the experience seemed so similar to what this counselor was describing as tongues. How could it be that the two phenomena were so alike, but one was holy and one was evil? I was trying to use thoughts to sift through a world that thinking was not made for, something beyond the realm of intelligence.

I was taught that my testimony was best kept emotional, experiential. When evangelizing, I was supposed to talk about how God healed me, changed my life, saved my soul in ways I could feel. Nobody could tell me that my experience was wrong. When I said *I feel*, they couldn't prove that I didn't.

I knew that speaking in tongues, the ability to access that mindset, would alter the secular world's perspective of me if I exposed it. I'd seen *Jesus Camp*. I knew how nonbelievers saw that level of spirituality. Maybe I had gained a level of spiritual intelligence through my discovery, entered a new realm of communion with God. But in the eyes of others, I would be seen as unhinged. Delusional. A person who fell for something, who was too stupid not to get trapped.

Yet I knew so many intelligent, accomplished people who bought into evangelicalism, who had intellectual reasons to do so, who saw something to occupy their vibrant minds. Scientists, philosophers, teachers, and entrepreneurs from every continent of the world, many of them highly educated and academically decorated, all convinced that belief in Jesus Christ as Lord and Savior was the one and only way to heaven. Joining the church, leaving the church—it's never about how "smart" or "stupid" you are. It's about where you're vulnerable, and what you need as a result.

✷

Becca found out I was having sex by accident. We had moved into an apartment with two other women from church. One night, we had our old roommate, Eleanor, over for dinner, and, not realizing Becca didn't know, she let it slip.

"I thought he was just sleeping over," Becca said about Nick.

"Becca, I don't believe the same things you do anymore," I said.

She put down her half-eaten bowl of quinoa and squash. "I just don't even want to picture it. Why him? He's like a rat."

Of course Becca didn't like Nick. He was too gruff for her tastes. He didn't wear flannel like the guys she went to church with, didn't have a fashionable beard or tattoos climbing up his arms. He had an odd, off-color sense of humor. He didn't fit the mold of we had been taught was the essential shape of a romantic partner. I told myself that I liked him for exactly that reason.

But what I told myself was inconsistent, and I knew it as I formed my narrative, as I developed a new set of reasons for the way I was living my life. Sure, Nick wasn't perfect, but he was ultimately a good person. He had walls up, but he was with me for a reason. Maybe he didn't understand my past, the fact that I was involved in this faith system, but his comments about "stupidity" were just reactive—he was probably just hurt *for* me. And everything, all the comments about cheating on me, those were all jokes.

The church taught me that God saw sex as a covenant. When you have sex, you're spiritually entering into marriage. I had sex with Nick in part to prove the church wrong, to show them that I could have a good relationship *and* have sex before marriage. But I was, without realizing it, still playing by their rules, still living like sex bound me to a person.

✷

My brother Matt called on a Sunday morning to let me know our mother was in the hospital. Emily and Gillian had woken up to find the bathroom trashed, used tissues and cotton swabs all over the floor, the garbage can on its side in the corner. They found my mother upright in bed, talking to herself. She said a man was tap dancing on the ceiling.

"I think she's withdrawing from the pills," Matt said. "You need to come home."

I bought myself the first bus ticket I could find and got to Southbridge. When I arrived in my mother's hospital room, she was not her usual self, the woman who usually greeted me with a hug and five kisses.

"Hi, Mommy," I said.

She nodded.

"Are you surprised to see me?" I asked.

"Yes."

My sisters and I explained to her that she was sick and that I was going to spend the night in the hospital with her, but she didn't believe us—she didn't think she was in a hospital. She laughed and said she was fine, that she was looking forward to eating the "pickled pie" that someone named Debbie had made for her.

Gillian walked into the corner of the room and cried. I hugged her and told her that this could be a good thing in the long run. It could mean no more pill addiction. It could mean our mother finally getting help.

I didn't sleep that night. Every few minutes, my mother would try to get out of bed, twisting her IV around her arm so she could "go hide in the dugout." She had me call my father at four in the morning because there were women on the wall in front of her.

"They're shaking their booties!" she screamed into the phone.

"Oh no," my dad said.

"Call Father John!"

"Okay, honey. I will."

She didn't fall asleep until eleven the next day, my entire family surrounding her, holding her hands, telling her to rest. When she woke up at nine the following morning, she was herself again.

"I'm in the hospital?" she asked.

We learned she had tried to lower her doses herself, safely, using her thirty years of nursing knowledge. But no amount of experience, no amount of intelligence, was going to keep her mind from going into the state it did. She could not outsmart her own addiction.

"I was trying to do it myself," she told us eventually, after an outpatient rehabilitation program. "I wanted it to go away quietly."

It turned out so differently from how the church told me it would. They predicted Jesus would save my mother, that if I prayed, if I devoted myself to God, he would bring my family around to faith. My mother's addiction could be a tool.

Now I saw her autonomy instead.

She picked up cooking, decorating, early morning walks with my father. I saw the pain drain from her eyes, an air of confidence replacing it. A belief that the world was not attacking her took hold. Some new vices replaced the old addiction—shoe shopping, deal seeking, everything to excess. When I visited on weekends, she'd have fifteen loaves of pumpkin bread already in the freezer as she started baking a new one.

My father shrugged. "At least it's not pills," he said.

I knew he was right, and I was proud of her for that. Or was I proud of God? Should I be thanking him? Was I wrong to think my mother saved herself?

*

Shortly before Thanksgiving, I was scheduled to perform a reading of some of my childhood journals for a show called *Mortified*. I worked with the producers to build a story out of my Prince Harry entries, culminating in a performance of a song I wrote for him when I was twelve. It was going to be a night of cathartic embarrassment, and I wanted Nick to be there to meet the person I once was—that intense, imaginative, ambitious-beyond-all-reason preteen.

He told me he was on his way, but never texted to say he'd arrived. After the show was over, I went into the audience to look for him, but I didn't see him anywhere.

"I don't think he came," Becca said.

"Not possible," I said. "He was on his way."

I called. Texted.

He finally called back around midnight, when I was lying in bed, my nose clogged from crying. "Sorry," he said. "I was entertaining some people from work."

"Who on earth did you need to entertain?"

"Some girls who were in town from Chicago. My boss wanted me to hang out with them."

"Why didn't you tell them you had plans?"

He told me that he was trying to impress his boss and get in good at the company.

"Do you even care about me?" I asked. "Do you even want to be with me?"

"You know how much I care about you," he responded in a tender voice that I hadn't heard since we first kissed, since he first held my hand like he wouldn't let go. "You know."

It wasn't unfamiliar territory, being told to believe the opposite of my experience. I settled into his words and created a story to hold on to, a story that said, despite his actions, he still wanted a relationship with me.

I told myself that story again when he held my head under a pillow until I had trouble breathing, a moment of playful wrestling that turned frightening, violent. He released me after a minute, saw my wet cheeks.

"You hurt me," I said.

"No, I didn't." He hugged me from behind. "No, I didn't."

I told myself that story when I forgot my birth control at his place and had to come back later in the day to grab it. "Don't want to get pregnant," I said.

"If you did, I'd throw you down the stairs."

I smirked and turned to him. "No, you wouldn't."

He was still, looking me in the face, blank. "Yes, I would," he said.

I told myself that story when I tried to leave a toothbrush in his bathroom for when I spent the night at his place. I didn't want to leave it on his sink, because what if that made him angry? What if he considered it a signal that I was stealing his space, trying to move myself in before he was ready? To be safe, I put it in the cabinet under his sink.

He walked into the bathroom, saw me close the cabinet door. "Are you snooping in my stuff?" he asked.

"What? No."

"Get the fuck out of my things."

He stomped around the apartment screaming that I needed to keep my nose out of what didn't belong to me.

I burst into tears. "I wasn't snooping," I said. "I was trying to keep it out of your way."

"Well, tell me that," he said. "Don't just go into my shit. How would you like it if I did that to you?"

I answered honestly. "If you looked under my bathroom sink, I wouldn't care."

The night he broke up with me, we were watching television. A blonde woman in shorts appeared, and he made some remark about wanting to have sex with her.

"Really?" I said. "You think these jokes are funny?"

"Are you kidding me?" he said. "You could have sex with any guy that walked through the door and I wouldn't care!"

I had broken a rule: I had expressed anger at something he said. I was silent for a few moments, collecting myself for a rational response. "It really hurts when you joke about cheating on me," I said.

He sighed. "I think we should see other people."

How did I let a person treat me the way Nick did? How did I let him convince me I was the one who needed to apologize? How was I stupid enough to stay with someone who threatened to throw me down the stairs, who almost suffocated me under a pillow, who joked about cheating on me in lieu of conversation? How was I dumb enough to want someone like him, to think this constituted a functioning, healthy relationship? Did wanting someone who called me stupid mean I actually was stupid?

I had lost the thread of who I was long before I met him. I was buried by the rules of evangelical Christianity and when he replaced them with a new set of rules, it felt so familiar I didn't notice. They were heavy, but I was used to carrying that kind of weight. I was used to calling myself the bad one and doing all the work to fix a relationship with someone who didn't reciprocate my love.

✷

I couldn't find my cat Libby the other day. I had a feeling she was trapped. I called her name from the kitchen as I opened a can of food and scooped it onto her plate.

She's probably just hiding, I thought. *Your anxiety is talking.*

No, I thought again. *She's trapped.*

I searched the apartment for her. She wasn't under the bed. She wasn't behind the curtain, no white paws under closet doors. I went back to the food.

She'll appear when I put it down, I thought.

No. You have this feeling. Look harder.

My mind went to the recliner, the one she occasionally chooses over me. *Is she stuck underneath?*

I walked over, got on my knees, and pulled the leg rest up. There Libby was. She had trapped herself inside.

Am I stupid to wonder if there's something a little mystical about such feelings? Do belief and hope have to equal stupidity? Am I stupid to give credence to anything supernatural? Am I stupid because it hasn't all gone away?

Fundamentalist belief is about exploited vulnerabilities, and fundamentalism comes in more forms than religion. You can find it in relationships, addictions, a fear of changing your ways. It can be the anger you detonate to keep people from getting too close.

But I do not believe that all belief is fundamentalist. I think there's a lot of mystery that holds our minds in its hands. I used to find it important to define and understand it. I don't anymore, and that is a great relief.

✷

In early 2014, I told my mother I had left evangelicalism. I walked thirteen blocks away from my apartment before I called so Becca wouldn't overhear. She put the phone on speaker when I told her I had important news. She wanted my father to hear.

"I stopped going to church," I said. "I don't believe in it anymore. It feels like I woke up from a dream."

I had been slowly waking up for the past two years—the subtle realizations, the small steps into the secular world, the crushes, the weed, the questions that couldn't be answered. Then the vomiting, the sleeplessness, when I tried to stay the course. My insides screaming, *Wake up. Stop this.*

This was a phone call my mother had predicted at least five years prior, when I sat on the foot of her bed and told her she needed to accept Jesus. "I think this is a phase," was what she said, and no assertion could have made me angrier.

"You're wrong," I said back then. "This is forever."

You are changed forever. The words of Cate. *People will tell you this is a phase. Don't let them fool you.*

My mother's reaction wasn't unlike one of those Publisher's Clearing House commercials where they surprise someone with an oversized check, but she tried to contain her joy, not wanting to frighten me away. My father, on the other hand, didn't say a word, overcome by shock and relief that this season of our lives was over.

I shared with them only the intellectual parts of what had brought me to that point. The inconsistencies, the issues with a literalist reading of the Bible, the problems that arose with the doctrine of infallibility. I shined a flashlight down the tunnel of evangelical thought I'd crawled out of, let them see how sticky it was, why it took me so long to leave it.

My mother soaked it all in. "You're going to be so much better for this. Oh my God, what you've seen. You're going to be so evolved."

She was speaking about a future I couldn't yet imagine.

20.

"You're going to be so much better for this" is what I tried to hear in my head after Nick broke up with me, as I blubbered all over the streets of New York, floating between apartments and bars, trying to bide my time in grief. What I told myself would be a forever relationship had turned out to be anything but, and for good reason.

He was abusive, I reminded myself. *I shouldn't want him back.* I *should have broken up with* him.

But that knowledge didn't remove the longing. He was a sort of rebound relationship for me after breaking up with Jesus. His behavior, however malevolent, felt familiar, like a home. Did I have the ability to take care of my own life? Could I make rational decisions? Could I trust myself with myself? I wasn't sure, but I was all I had—for that moment, for forever.

Evangelicalism didn't have to be forever. Neither did every romantic relationship. I began to understand these sentiments at a Friday night happy hour, when I kissed someone for the first time after I broke up with Nick. He was an ex-Catholic, and we talked about what it meant to leave our faith behind. For the first time in over a year, I was being spoken to like a human being by someone I was attracted to. We made out by the Second Avenue subway stop, and took each other's numbers before going home for the night.

The next day, I texted him. *It was great meeting you last night. :-)*

He answered back. *I really enjoyed meeting you too!*

After that, I didn't hear from him again.

I asked myself if I was upset that that kiss didn't become a full-blown relationship. What if it was just a lovely moment outside of a subway stop and that was enough? My idea of forever expanded—a moment could be forever. This moment could become a story to tell myself when my confidence waned: *You're not unattractive. Someone nice wanted to kiss you!* It could help me grow out of habitual ways of thinking that kept me stagnant, past-focused. *You can move on as many times as you want. No one person or thing has to be the whole of your world.*

With that mindset, I made myself a profile on some dating apps and entered a world my secular friends had long been a part of. I talked to people, agreed to meet up in public places. I learned to show up fifteen minutes early and buy my own first drink, giving myself the sense of agency I needed to feel comfortable leaving within half an hour if I wanted to. I decided to have sex if I wanted, on the first date or on the third, because sex, I learned, didn't have to be a big deal. It didn't have to be forever.

✷

Will was unhappy I had begun dating so soon after my breakup with Nick.

It's only been a month, he texted me. *Don't you think you should give yourself more time?*

I've spent enough time being single, I replied.

His distance from me had become more pronounced now that he was married to a woman he'd met at Pastor Luke's church. Will had wanted me to be a groomswoman, but his evangelical mother forbade it. Instead, I read a scripture and gave a short toast, the Christmas lights in the trees around us sparkling through my glass of champagne. In the days since, I hadn't seen much of him. The nights of hanging out on a whim were over. When I went to his house to announce my apostasy to him and his wife, they didn't seem to care. "If you're telling us you're okay," he said, "then we believe you're okay." I wondered if they'd had a discussion before I came, consulted with Pastor Luke, decided on an approach that would keep me connected to them by a thread in the hopes of one day reeling me back in.

Will had been one of my only sources of solace, but as time went on, he refused to journey with me down certain paths. When the topic of sex arose, he asked me point blank if Nick and I had done the deed.

Yes, I answered, even though I knew it was a response he wouldn't like.

Well, you're going to regret that one day, he replied. *Trust me. I did.*

He insisted I would learn that sex before marriage was too risky. I told him that yes, it had been painful, but I had learned about myself through the process, and ultimately, I was glad I had taken that risk.

I give it six months, he said. *You'll feel differently.*

Well, I guess we're different people, I said.

I stood my ground, shaking inside. I thought about my ability to do what I wanted with my body, and how Will would take that away from me if he could. What right did he have to dictate my sex life? What right did he have to evaluate a decision that was so deeply personal, that had nothing to do with him?

What was Will's role in my life now, anyway? In flashes I saw our friendship, those first moments at The New School, the beer and milkshakes, the brownie bake-offs, the endless hours of conversation. I grew and changed beside him. I was a better person for him. My best friend. I would have stayed his best friend forever, but we now lived in different worlds. We'd become different species. For me, his atmosphere was poisonous.

*

My relationship with Becca was also struggling. "I don't understand how you got so attached to Nick," she'd say. "I warned you about him, you know." We fought over trivial things, like whose turn it was to buy toilet paper and readjusting the seat on a bicycle. It was unexpressed frustration, I knew, at the predicament we found ourselves in—that we had become incompatible.

When we finally sat down to talk about it, Becca told me I had offended her.

"How?" I asked.

"Because I told you Nick was bad. And you didn't take my advice. You kept dating him anyway."

"This wasn't about you," I told her. "This was my relationship. It didn't revolve around you and things you said."

She took a breath, about to retort, words forming in the back of her throat. And then a light ignited in her eyes. "Oh!" she said. She had begun to understand that my decision to have sex was not an indictment of her personal wisdom.

We hugged before we went to bed that night, but I couldn't stop hearing the words "You didn't take my advice." I couldn't get over the fact that this friend of mine needed me to explain she had no business being offended by my breakup with someone else.

Yet I knew her behavior stemmed from evangelical teachings. *Be a woman of wisdom. Be accountable to one another. Submit to the authority of the Bible and its teachings.* The pastors who taught her these things were trying to help her lead a righteous life, but instead they stunted her as a human being, tearing away her ability to be a good friend.

Leaving evangelicalism, it seemed, had matured me. But staying in it had robbed Becca of empathy, the ability to see things from a different point of view. I could not save her from that.

✷

I sat across from many people for the very last time, people I knew I would love until the life inside me ended. It happened at restaurants and on park benches, in places too normal to expect such extraordinary endings. "I broke up with Nick," I'd say. "It hurts. I'm wading my way through the pain." The silence. The downward stares. I could read their minds, because they had all been trained to think the same thing. *You shouldn't have had sex with him*, their lack of words said. I could no longer stay in relationships where I was thought of in that way.

The evangelical community that once surrounded me was large—hundreds of church members, four years' worth of Campus Crusade kids. I had made more friends, gained more mentors, than I knew how to handle in this exit. Leaving evangelicalism was like a massive breakup, and I didn't have the strength to formally break up with every person—to explain to them that I was leaving their faith, and I wasn't taking them with me.

When it came to breaking up with Cate, I chose silence.

I remember the last time she called. I was at work, my phone buzzing beside my hand. We'd last talked a year prior, and I had hoped I wouldn't hear from her again, that she would simply disappear without me having to say a word—but here was her name on my phone's screen. *Missed call: Cate. Voice message: Cate.*

How do you end a relationship that almost killed you, that sought to replace your entire soul, exchanging the foundation of your very being with a white man's interpretation of a two-thousand-year-old ghost?

"Hey," the voicemail said. "I don't know if this is still your number. If it is, it's been a long time. I wanted to know how you're doing. I miss you. I love you." Her voice split. "Bye."

She will not be at my wedding. She will not be the godmother of my children. They will not call her auntie, or know much of her existence. She has disappeared from my present and will not exist in my future, though her memory will continue to evoke the strangest guilt, the feeling of disappointing a mother and, in some ways, a lover.

✷

After breaking up with Nick, I began dating like a maniac. I was having a grand old time, learning about sex, what felt good for me, as well as trying to figure out what I wanted in a partner. Why shouldn't I date a bunch of people at once? Why shouldn't I take advantage of the fact that I was finally allowed to explore my body, by myself, with other people?

It began on OkCupid. His profile read, *I hate needles and therefore hate bees because bees are flying needles.* This guy was clearly my type of weirdo. He messaged me that night, something about sci-fi and *Lord of the Rings*, which meant he had read my profile, too. When he asked me out, he suggested we go to a bar called the Waystation, because we were nerds and it was a nerd bar, with a bathroom decorated like a TARDIS from *Doctor Who*.

I'm running late. I texted. *Don't get there too fast!*

He texted back in seconds: *Okay! Currently walking backward.*

His name was Jason. When I arrived, he turned around on his barstool to face me and held out his arms, as if he were presenting himself. I shook his hand formally, like we were about to conduct a business meeting, and for the first time in a while, I let my date buy me a drink.

"Gin and tonic," I said.

"That's what I'm having!" he said.

It was early and the place was empty, so we sat across from each other in a horseshoe-shaped booth large enough for eight people. I felt like I needed the space to evaluate this person, let myself see him at a distance. When he stood up to get us another round, I invited him to sit back down next to me.

"Oh, I can sit next to you?" he said with a smile, and I nodded, patting the seat beside me, tipsy.

I kissed him that night in the middle of a sentence, my palm against his chest, right over his heart. We spent a good hour making out and drunkenly showing each other all the pictures on our Facebook profiles, catching up on all the years of our lives the other hadn't been there for. I felt like I had met a counterpart, someone who understood me, who wanted what I wanted and thought the way I thought. It was, oddly, a spiritual experience.

I went into the TARDIS bathroom and looked in the mirror at the lipstick fading off my lips, drunk on gin and affection.

"I think I just met my next boyfriend," I said to myself.

What I meant was "husband," but I avoided saying it, because I knew the disappointment of losing forever.

21.

Since leaving evangelicalism, I've come to realize how strongly it is designed to make people want to go back to it, particularly in moments of personal instability. With its robust community of followers, the faith opens a gate into a world of comfort and understanding if you profess the simple password of its fundamentalist belief. It is so fulfilling in its full-bodied, complex system of support that it is only natural to experience emptiness upon leaving it. I could never escape God because God made the rules of salvation. If I accepted him once, I accepted him forever. I was trapped in his love. He would not let me go. This type of trap, I believe, is an intentional aspect of any cult structure.

The temptation to return, to rest again in God's arms, to hear the messages of hope and love and inspiration, was powerful after my relationship with Nick ended. I was wading through a brand-new environment of romantic relationships and decisions, the gray areas of living a secular life, with none of my evangelical friends there to tell me I was special, to assure me I was making the right decisions. No prophecies, no prayers, no words of affirmation. Just me, trying to build a new life with nonbelievers. I missed the comforts of absolutes.

One of the most alluring things about Campus Crusade had been its staff: real, live adults for us to admire and emulate. They shared their life stages with us—their marriages, their decisions to have children, the preparations they made to have them dedicated to the Lord. I had examples before me, modeling how to handle any situation, from the most innocuous to the most difficult—people who could, and would, talk me through anything.

This was not something I had grown up with. I saw my parents as almost the opposite of role models; I recognized the ways in which they were unhappy, and in them I saw an adulthood I didn't want to mimic. How do you become an adult when your examples feel like chaos, the opposite of thriving? Evangelical Christianity stepped in, offering to grow me, reparent me, if I gave Jesus my life. Part of the grief of leaving was losing those examples, emptying the space they occupied and having to refill it on my own.

Without that unwavering support system, I wasn't sure how to process what happened to me, how to connect and share the trauma of my experience with others. I found myself unable to talk to others about normal things that didn't involve evangelicalism. "Hi! I'm Beth. I work in advertising, and I recently found my way out of a fundamentalist cult! How are you? I'm fine. Just trying to wrap my head around the fact that God's not sending everyone at this party to hell."

The people who were now around me didn't know how to respond—how could they if they hadn't experienced something similar? I rendered brunch tables speechless, picnics quiet.

People don't want to hear about this, I told myself. *People don't care how many years it took you to have sex.* Still, I yammered, the details involuntary. My mind was on a loop, a hamster on a wheel. I was processing a breakup with a whole way of life. There wasn't much room in me for anything else.

People in the secular world, I realized, were cagey, less open to sharing their life experiences, less willing to bare their hearts at the drop of a dime, mainly because they didn't know me, and thus couldn't really trust me. There was no spirit of Jesus, no theology that tied us together, no promise that we shared something beyond the common fact of our humanity. My openness did not inspire openness—if anything, it created discomfort. *Why is this girl I just met telling me about the time an interviewer made her admit to masturbating?*

I missed what I had, but I could not have it again. I would not go back. No matter how lonely it got, no matter how great the pain, I would not give up my newfound freedom for the effortless comforts of my former community. The price was my life, and that was far too much to pay.

*

By the spring of 2016, I was earning enough at my advertising job to move into a one-bedroom apartment by myself. Jason came over the night I moved in, my mattress on the floor, boxes completely unpacked. He surveyed the space in wonder, from the butler's window to the kitchen to the living room, the fresh hardwood on the bedroom floor. "Damn!" he said. "All right!"

We had been dating for eight months at that point, but he still wasn't ready to be "official." He was cool with spending weekends together and making me tea when I was sick. He was up for meeting my friends and helping me move. He just wasn't ready to call me his partner. So I performed both of our parts, and my arms were getting tired. I couldn't keep carrying whatever it was on my own.

Without a predetermined biblical frame to fit them into, I spent a lot of time analyzing my feelings. What exactly was so painful about his refusal to call me his girlfriend? Was it the label? Would I be fine if his parents knew about me? If we started spending holidays together, would I care what he called me—his special friend? His sandwich? His orange traffic cone? No, I didn't care about the label. I cared about the time, the treatment, the way I fit into his life. I wanted meaning beyond our immediate environment, our favorite restaurants in Brooklyn. I was ready for an adult relationship.

I didn't have an example for this. Neither the evangelical nor the secular world had an approved pattern for what I was doing. I was a woman pursuing a man, sticking around despite his hesitation, despite the fact he didn't seem ready. If the roles were reversed, I thought, if I were a man pursuing an indecisive woman, I'd be perceived as sweet. Patient. But as a woman sticking around for a man, I felt foolish. I was not guarding my heart, like the evangelical world had taught me to. I was not respecting myself, like some women's magazine would have told me to.

So I decided to tell Jason what I wanted, no matter the outcome. I sat with him on my mattress, heart palpitating, knowing that I'd say goodbye if we couldn't take this next step.

"I want to meet your parents," I said. "I'm ready for them to know me."

And as if he were expecting it, Jason nodded. "Okay."

✷

I remember giving up the fantasy of my angel family unwillingly. "There is a real God," Cate said, "and this story in your head isn't of Him. You are not the daughter of the angel Gabriel. You're a child of God himself. I am too, and so is everyone in this room. You can't back up this story in your head with the Bible."

She was right, I couldn't. I would miss the fantasy, but I would replace it. I would reinvent my heaven. It was convenient, in a way, to be able to keep God, even if he was a different God than the one I had believed in before. So I put my angel family in a mental closet, rid myself of any spirituality that didn't match evangelicalism's reading of the Bible. No Wicca, no karma, no reincarnation. No choice between heaven and a new life on earth after death. Nothing but salvation through faith in Jesus Christ.

When I went running out of evangelicalism, there was no time to grab my old beliefs. I left any certainty in heaven behind, the soothing God of my childhood dormant in the dark. Angels, spirits, all are inaccessible. I have seen too much to rationalize their existence. I have not found a substitute for the comfort of heaven, for a belief in the afterlife, for the peace that comes with knowing there's another phase. I don't know where we go when we die, and I used to know exactly where that was.

✷

It took several years not to feel like I was missing, like the world was passing by without me in it. Not to look at social media posts and wonder why they seemed to be from a society that had evolved beyond me, a time I wasn't living in. It took me that long to feel that I was living a real life. When you are told so persistently that leaving something will kill you, a part of you goes on believing it—involuntarily, because when it comes to indoctrination, choices are made for you.

When I was six years old and racked with separation anxiety at school, my mother gave me her ring on a chain to wear around my neck. I'd rub it and imagine it on her finger, and it helped me stop missing her. I have to hope that evangelicalism didn't fit me with a necklace too, that I will not look down one day to see it again around my neck. I have to hope that I am mostly free, that nothing about me is missing, that my survival thus far means that I am whole and was whole all along.

✷

I met Jason's parents a month later (at his sister's wedding—no pressure).

Two months later, he met my family. ("Dad, I'm warning you now, Jason is not going to want to watch you take the washing machine apart.")

Two weeks after that, as we were falling asleep, Jason surprised me again.

"Hey," he said into my hair, holding my waist from the back.

"What's up?"

"I love you."

Was I dreaming? Was he drunk? After all his hesitancy, how did the word *love* just pop out of his mouth? *Love.* It was the most overused word in the evangelical world. I heard it from strangers. I said it to people I didn't particularly like. I had to. God's command. We were family.

"I love you too," I said, then turned to him, accusatory. "Why did you say that to me?"

"Because I wanted to."

"Why? When did you decide? What made you say it?"

"I had an epiphany after meeting your family," he said. He told me about his last girlfriend, the isolation of their relationship. They began dating when he was sixteen and broke up just before he turned twenty-three. He spent some of his most formative years committed to this person, holed up emotionally, unable to participate in normal friendships. He didn't travel abroad in college because he was too worried about how she would fare a country away from him. "I realized that I've been scared the same thing would happen with you," he said. "That if I called you my girlfriend, we'd isolate ourselves and I'd lose my freedom and all these things I've learned about myself."

It was a fear I understood. I, too, had been isolated in a relationship, in a hundred relationships all at once. I, too, had been a prisoner of my own immaturity—my inability to grow past a life stage that didn't want to let me go. I, too, had recently entered into a life that felt normal, and I didn't want to lose that freedom either.

That night, we talked about what we wanted in a richer way than we could have spoken a year earlier. What made us compatible, what we needed, and how we knew. His reasons were secular, mine religious. His were, in some ways, easier for people to understand—what's not to understand about having a bad ex, about the shards of a past relationship?

Me?

"I'm God's ex-girlfriend," I said. "Maybe people will get it better that way."

Acknowledgments

I avoided writing this book for a long time, and I am incredibly grateful for those in my life who wouldn't let me keep doing that. To Rene Steinke, thank you for being the first to even say the word "memoir" and for helping me find both the courage and the vision to pull this into a real, live book—from those initial conversations to some of the earliest drafts. To Minna Proctor, thank you for answering every email about how the hell one goes about sending a book into the world and for pointing me in all the right directions, all while helping me distill everything I wanted to say into a coherent query.

To Kailey Roberts, thank you for being the president of my fan club and letting me send you chapters as I finished them (and for always reading them in under ten minutes and delivering helpful, encouraging feedback before I sat down to write again.) To my beta readers: Caitlin Elizabeth Harper and Suzanne Reisman, thank you for letting me test this book out on your incredibly astute eyes and for delivering the kind of support that made it impossible for me to give up on it after. To Lauren O'Neal, thank you for giving this book one of the best edits I've ever seen in my life and then becoming a fierce advocate for it. You are the kind of editor that makes writers want to keep writing.

To Anne Nelson and Katherine Stewart, thank you for every ounce of help and advice you've had for this project and for giving me so many avenues to explore until it found its way to this point.

To Chrissy Stroop, thank you for always elevating my writing and for so thoughtfully getting it in front of as many eyes as possible– your help has been so vast that I may never be able to repay you, but I really hope I can one day!

To my parents, thank you for giving me the freedom to share my perspective and letting me know that you would love me both through it and for it. To my siblings, thank you for living at least 75 percent of this with me, forgiving me for aggressively trying to save you from hell, and still being excited to see this book on shelves.

And last but certainly not least: to Jason, the very first editor to touch this book, thank you for helping me structure this into a cohesive, healing narrative—and for being the healing force that carries me through every day.